harvaja	mister	خواجة
hel	cardomom seed, a spice	هل
lijajeh	a mare's family tree	لجاجة
huraj	saddlebag	خرج
keffyeh	Arab headdress	كفية
khan	inn or rest house for caravans	خان
madafe	village guesthouse	مضافة
maidan	(plural: *mayadin*) horse race or the arena where a horse race takes place	ميدان
marhaba	a blessing upon you	مرحبا
marhabtein	a blessing upon us both	مرحبتين
mukhtar	headman of Arab village	مختار
nargileh	Arab water pipe or hubble-bubble	نارجيلة
pitta	flat, round Arab bread	פִּיתָּה
rotel	about 6½ pounds	رطل
sabras	prickly pear (Arabic)	صبار
assalaam aleikum	peace be with you	السلام عليكم
seder	ritual meal held on the first night of Passover	סֵדֶר
shtetl	townlet whose inhabitants were mostly Jewish	שטעטל
tfadalu	please come in or please join in	تفضلوا
tzabar	prickly pear (Hebrew)	צָבָר
wadi	ravine, dry riverbed	واد
wali	Moslem shrine	ولي
Yahud	Jews (Arabic)	يهود
yallah	run	يا الله

*The translation of this book into
English was made possible through a
grant from the Adolf Amram fund*

The Jewish Publication Society of America
. . .
Philadelphia   5733 · 1973

Yehoash Biber

· · ·

Adventures in the Galilee

· · ·

translated from the Hebrew by

Josephine Bacon

· · ·

illustrated by Assaf Berg

Contents

* * *

Preface

. . .

During the days of the British Mandate, the Galilee area of Palestine was as wild and stormy as the Wild West was during the pioneering days of the United States. Living side by side were Arab and Druse farmers in their villages, wandering bedouins with their black tents, and Jews in kibbutzim (collective farms) and moshavim (individual farms). British Army camps and camps of the mounted Frontier Police were also located in the area. Two small towns, Tiberias and Safad, were the main centers of the region and were similar to the small towns of the Wild West.

The State of Israel was founded within the territory of Palestine in 1948, but Jews had lived in Israel many years before that. They had lived together with their Arab and Druse neighbors, often in peace and goodwill. They often got together to protect themselves against attacks from the robbers and desert-dwellers that roamed the area in those wild days.

In the Galilee they developed good relations and common customs. The Jews learned to speak Arabic and grew to know the habits and customs of their neighbors, and the Arabs helped the Jews. They visited each other. The Jews enjoyed the warm hospitality of the Arabs and the Druses, who admired the modern equipment that the Jews brought with them.

In those days the mare, the rifle, and the dagger were part of daily life, as were the black coffee prepared for visitors, the adventure stories told around the campfire, and the unique water pipe of the Arabs. *Adventures in the Galilee* tells something about those days.

You can read about the field guards who chased sheep rustlers exactly as the sheriff chased cattle rustlers in Arizona and Texas. You can read stories about the Arab and Druse peoples that were told around the campfire; about the bravery of the

Druses and the life of Jews; about noble steeds, camels, and naughty Yitzhak and his friends and their pranks. And finally there is a story of the first days of the State of Israel, called "Scout Plane over the *Wadi*," which is about another area of Israel, the Negev, that was as wild then as the Galilee had been before.

Y. B.

. . .

Adventures in the Galilee

1

· · ·

Sheep Rustlers

One night the largest of our sheep pens was broken into, and twenty head of sheep were stolen and driven off somewhere. Among the stolen sheep was Tumaleh, the leader of the flock. To our great shame, the watchman that night had been the famous Caruso himself, the best of our night watchmen. He had not realized that anything was amiss, and the thieves had made off with their booty right under his nose. This is how it happened:

It was a clear summer night. There was no moon, but the stars shone like little torches and shed

a pale glow. Caruso loosened the strap of his rifle—
it was cutting into his shoulder—and made his
umpteenth round of the farm buildings. From the
stable came the scrape of hooves, the rattle of
chains, and the peaceful sound of munching. The
cows flicked their tails against their legs and chewed
their cud, lowing mournfully from time to time.
The watchman approached the sheepfold and
glanced into its shadowy depths. The sheep had
huddled into one corner of the pen and were quieter
than usual.

"There's something bright over there in the
corner," mused the weary watchman to himself. "It
looks just like a *keffiyeh*—an Arab headdress." Then
he burst into loud laughter and said to himself,
"Aye, yay, yay, this watchman's job is making you
jumpy, pal! You're seeing things!" So he loosened
the strap of his rifle once again and made for the
lighted dining hall, to gulp down hot coffee and eat
the meal kept warm for the watchmen. While he
was eating and passing the time of day with the
dairymen, who had just finished the night milking,
the rustlers got busy. In the morning when the
shepherds arrived at work, they found that the
fence had been smashed, and the pride of the flock
had vanished.

"Dear, oh dear," mocked Mishke, the fat
shepherd, winking a twinkling eye. "It's a bad day

for the children of Israel when those who guard our fields become night watchmen!"

"Someone ought to be given the special job of watching the field watchmen, and that's that," added Motke That's That, so called because he ended every sentence with an emphatic "and that's that."

Meanwhile, other members had gathered at the spot and were making their contributions of advice and hypothesis.

"Don't spoil the tracks!"

"Hey, you there, move away from the fence! The trackers won't find a thing."

"The police should be alerted."

"Rubbish! Those lazy devils—they'll come here with their dog and find hot air. They'll find yesterday, but they won't find our sheep."

"It would be best to go and see Abu Yussuf," advised someone else. "Grease his palm, and he'll bring the robbers out from under the earth."

"But what if it was his own tribesmen who did the stealing?"

"Abu Yussuf is our friend!"

"Respect him but suspect him, as the saying goes."

"Nonsense!"

"Nevertheless . . ."

While they were still talking, arguing, and offering advice to each other, one of the brighter members had rushed off to wake the principal actor in this drama, Caruso, who was asleep in the watchmen's tent. The others stood around talking for a while longer and then hurried off to the dining hall to fill their bellies. After all, stolen sheep are one thing, but steaming hot coffee is quite another. While they were drinking, dunking thick slices of bread spread with jam, and stuffing their mouths with salad, the quick-witted kibbutz member had reached the watchmen's tent and was shaking the supine figure, whose head was wrapped in a towel to keep out the light and the flies.

"Caruso, wake up!"

"Go away. Let me sleep."

"Get up. The sheep . . ."

"Sheep, shmeep, I've only just gone to bed . . ."

"Listen, get up, they've stolen . . ."

"What have they stolen?"

"The sheep, they've stolen the sheep!"

"What!"

The watchman was on his feet in a flash. He sat down on the bed, his eyelids drooping with fatigue, his hair rumpled.

"Have they really stolen them? How?"

"They broke a hole in the fence."

"Are there any tracks?" he asked, already getting down to practical matters.

"Tracks? How could you trace their tracks?

The paths are covered with sheep tracks. You might as well look for a needle in a haystack."

"I'm getting up. In the meantime, go saddle Peter for me. Yes, and another thing. Tell Shai to take Knight. Arik isn't here today. He's gone off to attend a Haganah course. Shai is the only one who can ride Knight."

"All right, I'm on my way."

While Caruso gets dressed and goes off to see to the horses, I'll tell you a few facts you ought to know, because they have a direct bearing on the story.

None of us knew his real name. Everyone called him Caruso. Why? Well, one evening a young man came into view, strolling up the avenue of trees leading to the kibbutz and singing arias and songs from Italian operas at the top of his voice. This was how he entered the kibbutz gate, and he did not stop singing even then.

"Hey, fellows, listen to Caruso!" joked Yankeleh, the kibbutz comedian. So the young man was welcomed with raucous laughter. To his credit, he remained undaunted even by this rowdy welcome and calmly addressed himself to the kibbutz secretary. What those two talked about was and will remain a secret. The young man had been sent to us by the Haganah for reasons which are better left untold. In any case, our secretary became the possessor of two secrets: what the fellow was doing on our kibbutz and what his real name was.

From that day on, he was known to us all as Caruso. He did not try to stop us from calling him that. On the contrary, he rather seemed to like his nickname. At cookouts and parties he would give a solo performance, accompanied on the guitar by Arik, the other watchman. He would sing arias from famous operas, imitating Enrico Caruso, the famous Italian singer of that time.

All the kibbutz children liked Caruso. He had made friends with them within the first few days he was with us. This was mainly because he was a watchman in the fields, and this, in the young people's opinion, was the most important and most glamorous job on the kibbutz. But it was also because he was jolly and kindhearted and loved children. He would take them on long rambles into the fields and hills, and he would teach the older ones to ride his horse, Peter. Sometimes he would invite them all to the watchmen's tent, where he would give them a royal feast with aromatic coffee, prepared in true oriental style.

Shai, the oldest boy on the kibbutz, took a particular liking to the watchman. The pair went on many trips together, Shai riding Knight, a spirited and unruly horse. Shai had a special gift for handling horses. Only he and Arik, the other watchman, could ride Knight. Other people were frightened even to go near the horse, for he kicked and bit. Only the bravest showed Knight how clever they were by mounting him. However, the results were both unfortunate and comical—these heroes were unable to remain in the saddle for more than a second. Still, it may be better to draw a veil over these incidents, to avoid embarrassing friends and showing them up in public.

While we're on the subject of Caruso, let's not forget his brown horse, Peter, who had acquired a reputation as the best watchman's horse in Galilee. Peter had been bought from the British police and was remarkable for his rare qualities. He was swift and calm; his senses were keen; and he possessed amazing strength—in short, he was blessed with every virtue.

While Caruso is dressing, we still have a little time to talk about the thieves from the bedouin tribe of Arab-el-Haybe, who have a considerable part to play in our story, as we shall soon see.

The tribesmen were nicknamed "the Hebim." The tribesmen lived in an encampment of tents, which also contained a few stone houses, situated on a low hill south of our kibbutz. The place was called Tubas and was the site of a Moslem shrine, or *wuli*. Half these bedouin cultivated the land, and the rest were primitive livestock-raisers who grazed their black goats on other people's pastures. It was the enormous appetite of these goats that made it necessary for Caruso to guard the fields.

Yet if the truth be known the true occupation of these tribesmen was neither farming nor goat-breeding. Their sparse fields and handful of mangy goats were only a blind to conceal their real activities. Under cover of darkness, these daring horsemen would steal across the frontier and raid villages on the opposite side of the Jordan River, rustling cattle and sheep. Then they would ford the Jordan again and come back to sell their plunder in the cattle markets of Palestine. There were many bloody encounters between these robbers and the villagers, the border cavalry and the border guards. For this reason, the Hebim were hated by their fellow Arabs, and this is why they had established friendly relations with the *Yahud*—the members of our kibbutz.

Unfortunately, this friendship did not stop them from grazing their flocks in our clover and cornfields. Moreover, the tribesmen were in the habit of pilfering small items; they would pull washing off the line and hide it under their voluminous cloaks, or remove parts from machinery which had been left out in the fields, or cut ripe grain. Yet all these were simply petty thefts, too minor to disrupt friendly relations, and "misunderstandings" were always settled amicably.

The sheikh of the tribe, an elderly man with

a full beard and an imposing appearance, was named Abu Yussuf. (Arabs are usually known as "Abu So-and-so" meaning "the father of—" the name of their eldest son.) He rode a thoroughbred white mare whose saddle was decorated with multi-colored tassels, fringes, ribbons, beads, and shells; two embroidered pouches hung down on each side. He carried at his hip a Mauser pistol and a silver dagger inlaid with jewels and encased in a wooden sheath. His shoulders were draped with a brown striped silk cloak with a richly embroidered hem.

Abu Yussuf was treated with great respect by his acquaintances and was a welcome guest at the kibbutz. We would see him from afar, riding along the dirt track leading from the eucalyptus grove, and two of our Arabic-speaking members would immediately go to greet him and lead him to the room in which we entertained visitors. Here he would be served coffee, candy, and fragrant cigarettes. The old sheikh would drink the coffee, taste the candy, and savor the cigarette smoke.

Only after a lengthy conversation about matters completely unconnected with the purpose of his visit—his mares, his wives, the kibbutz harvest, various types of weapons and agricultural machinery, and so on—only after these things had been fully dealt with would the true purpose of the visit be revealed. Soon the sheikh would be clutching a goodly sum of *bakshish*—money—in his hand as a

bribe, the stolen goods would be returned to their owners, and everything would be settled peaceably. The sheikh's respectable appearance was misleading. His true character was turbulent and fiery. He was crafty, jealous, and unbelievably avaricious. Exaggerated stories of his exploits had given him an inflated reputation on both sides of the Jordan.

By now Caruso will have put on his shoes and buckled on his revolver; he will have even had time to swallow a cup of black coffee to chase away the vestiges of sleep.

His first step was to go and survey the scene of the crime. He examined the tracks around the fold with scrupulous care, sniffed here, smelled the ground there, and stood and compared, to the accompaniment of the jeers of Mishke and Motke, who had not yet taken the flock out to graze so they wouldn't trample the tracks.

"What a hero!" laughed Mishke, winking at Motke That's That. "If you had done a bit of guarding yesterday, you wouldn't have had to do any investigating today."

"That's right," agreed Motke. "You wanted to drink hot coffee, eh? You ought to have been on guard, and that's that," he concluded as usual.

The sun rose in the east and began to radiate its scorching heat. It was still only about 8 A.M., but the heat had already become oppressive. Caruso did what he had to, examined what he wanted to, and went off to the stable. There his horse awaited him, already saddled and bridled.

Shai stood next to Peter, tending the unruly Knight. He tightened the girth, fastened the bridle, and let out a whoop of joy. "Well, Caruso, are we going for a ride?"

"What—"

"Where to, Caruso?"

"Er . . . ," mumbled Caruso and refused to answer.

Caruso checked the girth and looked to see that the saddle blanket was in position, so that the horse's hide would not be chafed. He adjusted a strap by one more notch, tightened another knot, made everything ready for a long ride, and finally mounted. Shai followed suit, and the pair rode off into the sun-scorched fields of stubble, from which the grain had long since been harvested and which were now turning yellow.

Shai was in high spirits. After all, no one would turn up his nose at a chance to ride after sheep rustlers with the most popular watchman on the kibbutz! It would be quite an adventure. Shai tried to put on a serious expression, but he was unsuccessful. His heart was full of happiness, and he broke into a merry song.

They crossed the fields and reached the bridge, where they left the road and descended into the rocky, stony bed of the *wadi*, a dry riverbed.

The horses' hooves raised clouds of dust and gravel. Peter ambled along quietly as usual, but Knight skipped and leapt impatiently, longing to canter and breaking into an occasional whinny.

"Where are we riding, Caruso?" asked Shai.

"Mmmm . . ."

"Do you know where the sheep are?"

"I wouldn't say that."

"Well, then?"

"We have to do something, don't we?"

"Yes, but just to ride off somewhere . . ."

"Not just anywhere. Now listen," explained Caruso, marking off the points on his fingers. "Number one, the sheep weren't stolen before midnight . . ."

"So what?" interrupted Shai impatiently.

"That means the rustlers haven't gone far. They must certainly have hidden the sheep in the district. Two," he counted off on the next finger, "I believe the thieves are some of our friends the Hebim."

"How do you know?"

"I examined the area around the pen. The Hebim rustlers go raiding in rubber shoes. I saw prints of that type of shoe around the pen."

"Great. Let's ride off to their village."

"Certainly not. That's the whole point. Three, Abu Yussuf is clever enough not to hide the

thieves in the village. He is perfectly well aware
that a search will be made there."

"So where to?"

"That's what I don't know exactly."

"Well, then?"

"Four," and he counted off a fourth finger, "I
think the rustlers hid their loot near the Yarda
spring."

"How do you know?"

"If you had bothered to look where we are
going, without wasting your time staring up at the
empty sky, and if you had asked fewer questions,
you would know why yourself."

Shai looked shamefacedly downward. And
sure enough, the *wadi* path was covered with fresh
sheep droppings, showing that a flock had recently
passed.

"You see, Shai, this is not the usual path the
shepherds take. They would prefer to go along the
banks of the *wadi*. The going is much easier there."

"Yes, that's logical. That means they hid the
plunder in the *wadi*, eh?"

"Precisely."

A long time had passed. The saddles creaked
and gave off the pungent odor of heated leather and
horse sweat. The path became steeper and wound
between boulders as it began to cut through a steep
gorge. It reached the groves of Wuzia, then twisted
sharply and began to climb the hillside.

"Caruso!" called Shai. "The tracks continue along the *wadi.*"

"I know. But I am reconstructing the path taken by the robbers. I don't think they hid in the woods at Wuzia—they must have gone to the spring. They had to water the sheep, didn't they? Otherwise, they would all die of dehydration in the heat. You don't think the robbers want a load of carcasses on their hands, do you?"

"Of course not."

"We must hurry. If we find the loot by nightfall, the sheep will be safe. The robbers know the mountain paths well and will take their spoils a long way."

With a little more exertion, the horses reached the hilltop. Below them gushed the spring, surrounded by the thick green foliage of eucalyptus trees. The bed of the stream was outlined by the dark green leaves of oleander bushes. A few shepherds were watering their flocks around long wooden troughs.

"What bad luck," groaned Caruso. "Those flocks have obliterated the tracks."

"Yes, but they're goats. We're looking for sheep."

"Even so, it'll make things difficult."

The horses trotted down the slope. It was noon, and the heat was even greater. The sound of the cool water had reached their ears and increased their thirst. They began to canter impatiently down to the water.

"*Marhaba*—a blessing upon you!" Caruso greeted the shepherds.

"*Marhabtein,*" they answered. "May a blessing be upon us both."

After the customary formal exchanges, the pair loosened their saddle girths and sent the horses off to drink. The horses dipped their forelegs into the trough, splashed their necks, and drank thirstily.

Caruso was a familiar figure to the shepherds. Several of them had felt his strong arm when they had trespassed on the clover fields of the kibbutz.

"*Tfadal*—please join us," said the shepherds, inviting the pair to a modest meal of sour milk and dry *pitta*, which is Arab bread. Caruso seated himself cross-legged beside them, and the conversation began.

First came the customary inquiries after the well-being of the flocks. Had there been many lambs this year? Was the wool sufficiently abundant? Then the shepherds related how Ahmed's ewe had been carried off by a wolf and how Salim's had fallen into a pothole and broken a leg. Conversation then ranged to the topics of wives and children. Caruso knew each of the shepherds' children, and he inquired after them all by name.

Finally, the demands of courtesy having been met, Caruso asked the question which had been on the tip of his tongue all the while. "Has one of you shepherds seen twenty sheep in the vicinity?"

"Heaven forbid, *Hawaja* Caruso," the shepherds were quick to reply, adding weight to their affirmations by invoking the name of Allah, the great God, and by swearing oaths and solemn affirmations on the beard of the Prophet, on the eldest son of the shepherd Ahmed, on the wife of Salim, and on the devil's tail. The shepherds had seen nothing. They swore it by the great and wonderful Allah; not even the shadow of a ewe had been seen in the vicinity.

The time came for the two searchers to take their leave. Hands were shaken and blessings exchanged. The horses were saddled again and the riders mounted.

"*Salaam aleikum*—peace be with you!"

"*Aleikum salaam!*"

Caruso led Peter from the spring in the direction of the ancient *khan*, a rest house for caravans.

"Where to?" asked Shai.

"To the *khan*. Those wretched shepherds. Do you think they don't know? May their houses be destroyed! They know, and how they know! Not only do they know, but they actually helped the robbers by obliterating the tracks. Look, they have trampled all over the whole area with their flocks."

"That's true. All the paths are covered with tracks."

"What's more, the stolen sheep were led along the bed of the stream to make it more difficult to trace them. That crafty Abu Yussuf has made a good job of things this time!"

"What shall we do?"

"Trust Caruso. We are on our way to the *khan*. I am willing to bet my head that Abu Salim is mixed up in this affair. Nothing happens around here without his knowledge."

The *khan*, which was built of chiseled limestone blocks, stood on a high hilltop. Once, a long time ago, it had been an inn where travelers and their mounts could spend the night. Now it baked in the burning sun and was battered by the driving rain; weeds flourished among its ruins. The *khan* consisted of a large courtyard, entered by a rusty, squeaking iron gate. The courtyard was bounded on three sides by a low wall containing many empty, reeking stalls. On the fourth side of the courtyard, the southern side, stood a much higher building containing guest rooms, bedrooms, and a staircase leading to the flat roof. This is all there was to the mysterious *khan*.

Recently Abu Salim, an Arab watchman, had made his home in the deserted *khan*. The farmers of the Jewish settlement of Rosh Pina, who owned fields in the vicinity, employed Arab labor. Abu Salim, who was one of their workers, had been allotted the task of guarding the fields. Whether or not he was an efficient, loyal watchman is another matter.

In any case, since the *khan* was abandoned and anyone had the right to live there if he pleased, Abu Salim had left his bedouin tent and housed his few goats in one of the empty stalls, making another into a stable for his magnificent mare. He himself occupied one of the largest and most spacious rooms —he, his wives, his chickens, and his numerous offspring.

The Jewish youths in the neighborhood knew him well. When they went on rambles to the *khan*, he would come out to greet them, smiling warmly. *"Tfadal,"* he would say, "please enter and accept hospitality under my roof." Some would go in, drink the coffee which was always boiling on the fire in the middle of the room, and listen to a conversation between Caruso and the Arab watchman.

As Caruso and Shai toiled arduously up the steep hillside path leading to the *khan*, the track became steeper and more tortuous. Another twist, another turn, and yet another bend, and the big gate confronted them. From the entrance rushed a pack of mangy, diseased-looking dogs, barking madly at

them. The riders were undismayed. There is a saying that "a barking dog does not bite," and this is
even truer of an Arab dog. Arab dogs are mongrels,
the result of the mixing of a hundred strange
breeds. These dogs are degenerate and can't do
much harm. They are amazingly cowardly, but
they make excellent watchdogs because they are so
frightened of everything. Their ears are on the alert
for the slightest whisper, and they bark loudly
whenever anything approaches the bedouin's tent.

A boy ran out of the *khan*. Dressed in rags,
he was barefoot and dull-eyed. He threw a stone at
the dogs, sending them howling back into the *khan*.
This was Salim, the watchman's eldest son. The
dogs yelped in pain and reared back on their hind-
quarters; then they rubbed themselves fawningly
against the boy's legs. The pair dismounted. Salim
took the reins and tied the horses to a hitching-post.
Abu Salim was already waiting in the doorway of
his room, wrapped in a voluminous cloak, ready to
greet them. *"Salaam aleikum!"*

"Aleikum salaam!"

"Tfadal, please enter!"

Soft cushions were placed around the small
fire burning in the center of the room. The pair
removed their shoes and stepped onto the mat.
They seated themselves on one side of the fire, resting their arms on the cushions. Facing them sat Abu
Salim, barefoot and leaning on one elbow; with his

other hand he poked at the embers of the fire with iron rods. His first wife, a withered old crone, was cutting up green fodder for the chickens which ran freely about the room.

Abu Salim began the ceremonial preparation of the coffee, with all its elaborate detail. Coffee beans were placed in a small iron saucepan, which was heated over the fire until the roasting beans gave off a pungent smell. They were then poured into a small wooden mortar, and the host rhythmically beat them into a powder with a pestle. In the meantime, the guests sat and chatted with their host about this and that—the harvest, the flocks, thefts, the bedouin incursions called *azu*, and the watchman's latest wife, a girl aged fifteen, who was hiding all the while behind the curtain partitioning off the women's section. From time to time the curtain would twitch, and a pair of eyes burning with curiosity would peep out at the visitor.

The coffee grinding was completed. The fragrant powder was poured into a soot-encrusted copper coffeepot. The host added water, then sugar, to the pot and boiled the mixture on the hot embers. While the coffee was brewing, the host produced a few grains of *hel* (cardamom seed); no Arab coffee-making expert ever forgets to add these aromatic grains to his drink. Abu Salim crushed them in the mortar and added them to the pot.

The coffee boiled and bubbled, emitting a pleasant odor. The host poured it out into tiny china cups, which he served to his guests on a burnished brass tray. *"Tfadal."* Each guest took a little cup filled with the fragrant brew. They blew gently over the surface of the drink to cool it a little and drank it down noisily, praising their host, that he might live to prepare such a miraculous beverage for many long years to come.

Coffee was served two or three times, and then Caruso offered his host some excellent cigarettes. Only then did the conversation reach its climax, the reason for which the two were putting themselves to such trouble and had accepted Abu Salim's hospitality.

"May our generous host forgive us for the trouble to which we are putting him!"

"Oh, please, please. All the owner of this house desires is to serve his guests."

"It is a minor matter of little importance."

"Be it great or small, the host will do his utmost to satisfy his guests' desires."

"It is a minor matter of little importance."

"Whether great or small, the host will do all in his power to satisfy his guests' desires."

"It is a small thing, only the matter of a few stolen sheep, about twenty of them." Here Caruso used his two hands to show his host the exact number.

"The owner of this house would be happy to help you, but since yesterday I have not been feeling well. I have not even gone out to guard the fields. Salim, *ta'al hun!*" he called to his son, who confirmed his father's words, swearing a thousand oaths to the effect that his father was indeed ill and had not stirred beyond his threshold since the previous day.

"Perhaps, even so . . ."

"No, on the life of the host, no. A man like Abu Salim would not lie."

"Perhaps the thieves visited the *khan?*"

"Heaven forbid, they didn't show their noses in here."

"As you know, those who help detect thieves receive a considerable sum of *bakshish.*"

"Indeed, the head of this household knows the amount he is likely to receive if he finds the thieves, and despite his illness he is willing to saddle his mare and go out to help the searchers. But in vain. His help will be of no use. Nothing has been seen around here. By the life of Allah and by the beard of the Prophet!"

"In that case, there is no alternative. We must leave. Thank you for the coffee. The guests have taken great delight in the pleasant welcome they have received, but they have little time. Otherwise they would stay for many more hours under the host's roof."

"Please, please, his house is open at any time to such honored visitors, and everything he owns is theirs."

The horses were unhitched, and the pair mounted and rode out of the *khan*, accompanied by the pack of dogs and the smile of the watchman.

"Where to now, Caruso?"

"Trust me."

"Do you think that Abu Salim knows nothing?"

"Of course he does, and how! Nothing escapes the eyes of that old raven. He must have received a bribe from the thieves and helped them to hide the stolen sheep. What can one do? Their moral code is different from ours."

"Where to now?"

"To Cyclamen Hill."

"Cyclamen Hill? What for?"

"Perhaps the thieves hid their booty there. The hill is riddled with caves and hiding places. The Hebim are in the habit of concealing their plunder there until the hue and cry dies down."

"Aha!"

"It's midday already. If we don't find the flock quickly . . ."

"I understand."

The path dropped away steeply. Cyclamen Hill loomed before them. In the springtime the children would run off to the hill to pick the delicately perfumed, pale pink wild cyclamen, which grew in profusion among the rocks. This hill was pitted and honeycombed with caves. The path was sprinkled with sheep traces. Caruso dismounted and examined them.

"They're fresh," he called out.

"But there are so many of them—far more than could be made by twenty sheep. A large flock must have passed this way."

"That only increases my suspicions. They have trampled out the tracks with the herds of goats and sheep belonging to those shepherds."

"Look, here are some hoofprints!"

"That's it. I guessed it!"

"What did you guess?"

"That's Abu Salim's mare. Look at the hoofprint of the left front hoof. It is cleft. The courtyard of the *khan* is covered with hoofprints like those."

"Caruso, Caruso—why do they call you Caruso? I'd call you Hawkeye or Sherlock Holmes!"

"You learn by experience. All you need is a sharp eye and a good memory; then you'll be able to read tracks like a book."

While they were talking, they were drawing nearer to Cyclamen Hill. Flocks were grazing all over it, and it was hard to trace any definite tracks.

"Listen, Shai, we'll split up and carefully check each cave and crevice. You look along the path to halfway up the hillside. I'll examine it from there on. But be careful—the thieves are certain to be armed."

"O.K., Caruso. Come on, let's start."

For two hours the pair examined every nook and cranny and every cave in the mountainside, with no luck. Though the sun began to sink in the west, it still burned down fiercely.

"It's no good," sighed Caruso when the two eventually met up again. We must think of some sort of trick."

"Listen, Caruso, I've got an idea!"

"Come along, then. Let's hear it!"

Before we hear Shai's idea, I must explain who Tumaleh was. One day at dusk, Mishke, the shepherd, led the flock back from the pasture, carrying a small, delicate ewe lamb across his broad shoulders.

"What happened, Mishke?"

"This lamb was born in the field."

"And the mother?"

"Died while giving birth."

"Poor thing! What will you do with the motherless lamb?"

"Oh, I expect I'll get lots of advice."

Every evening the children of the kibbutz

would run along the path to meet the shepherds and help them herd the sheep into the pen. Shai was among them. "Listen, Mishke, give her to me," he begged.

"Are you crazy? What for?"

"The Education Committee has decided that we children are to have our own pets' corner. So far, all we have are chickens and rabbits. We have a lot of pens and hutches but nothing to go in them. They are all empty. Give us the lamb. We'll look after her."

"And you youngsters will bring her milk?"

"Of course. Every day!"

"And you'll pad the pen with straw?"

"Yes, we will!"

"And you'll clean out the pen?"

"Yes, we'll clean it."

"Well, then, take her. But be careful. She's small and still very young. She's only just been born."

"Don't worry, Mishke, we'll look after her as if . . . as if . . . as if she were a baby, O.K.?"

"All right—take her away and be off with you."

That is how the lamb reached the children's pets' corner, where she lived in a small wooden pen. They called her Tuma, or Tumaleh as an affection-ate nickname. Tuma grew up well and strong. She loved all the children, but Shai more than anyone else. She would stick to his heels like a well-trained, faithful dog. "Tuma, Tuma, Tuma," he would call, and she would come running immediately to her protector and follow him wherever he went.

When she grew into a sheep, she was returned to the kibbutz flock and became its best leader. She was used to human company. She obeyed every command, and ran after the shepherd with the whole flock following her. That's the way sheep are—a foolish race, blindly following their leader wherever he goes. Yet even when Tuma was leader of the flock, she did not forget Shai; she remained faithful to him. When he called her, she would abandon her new masters and come running to him. More than once, Shai, the practical joker, would send the flock into confusion and panic in order to provoke the shepherds: Mishke, who was easily angered, and Motke That's That. Mishke must have often regretted having given the lamb to the impudent Shai.

"*Nu,* open your mouth and speak up," urged Caruso.

"Tumaleh was one of the sheep."

"Huh?"

"You know how she adores me."

"So what?"

"So, I'll call to her."

"I see. And then she'll come out of the cave and give her position away?"

"Exactly!"

"O.K., go ahead. Only, let's hope that the thieves don't stop her from showing herself."

The campaign was planned down to the last detail. Shai began to search the mountainside, calling, "Tumaleh, Tumaleh, come here . . . come here" at the top of his voice.

He rode the length and breadth of the hill, followed by Caruso, whose eyes raked the hill. They rode and called for a long time, but without result. When they had almost given up in despair, they passed behind a spiky jujube plant and found a narrow ravine in the hillside. Suddenly, they heard a thin bleating, and a gray sheep broke out of one of the caves and ran straight up to Shai.

"Here she is!" exclaimed Shai joyfully. "Here's my Tumaleh!"

In a flash, Caruso had drawn his revolver and had ridden up to the mouth of the cave, which appeared to be empty. He shouted loudly, *"Etlauw, ya shabaab—*come out, boys!"

There was no answer, no sound. The cave was silent as the grave.

"*Etlauw!*"

Still no reply.

"It's no good," muttered Caruso. "I'll have to bring them out by force."

He cocked the revolver and fired a few warning shots into the air. The report of the revolver split the silence and echoed in the surrounding valleys. Then a loud whispering was heard, and two men wrapped in long cloaks and wearing rubber shoes rushed out of the cave, brandishing daggers. When they saw the revolver, they stopped and raised their hands. They were both Abu Yussuf's men.

"Shai!"

"Yes, Caruso?"

"Go into the cave," instructed Caruso. "But be careful. Take my flashlight."

Shai jumped from his horse, took the flashlight, and entered the cave. Soon he let out a triumphant shout. "Caruso! They're all here, all nineteen of them!"

"Excellent, Shai. Bring them outside."

Using a stick and his voice, Shai brought the frightened sheep out of the cave. Caruso sat impassively on his horse. He nonchalantly searched his trousers pocket and brought out a pack of cigarettes. Selecting a cigarette from the pack, he stuck it in his mouth and lit it calmly, as if nothing else

was occupying his attention. Suddenly, before the two Arabs or Shai understood what was happening, he cocked his revolver and fired wildly into the air.

"You wretches—be off, before I tear your filthy heads from your bodies! *Yallah*—run!" Bang, bang! Caruso fired his revolver again. Only when the two robbers had disappeared behind the mountainside did Caruso break into a hearty laugh.

"Well, Shai, what did you think of that *fantasia*, that exhibition?"

"Wonderful. But why didn't you capture them and take them to the police?"

"It's not worthwhile spoiling relations with Abu Yussuf. We have made them look silly enough by having discovered their plan. Now, get on your horse again. The sun is nearing the mountains in the west, and we have a long way before us yet. *Yallah!*"

And this is how they rode back: Shai led the way on Knight, loudly caroling popular songs. To tell the truth, his voice wasn't too musical; in fact, even the sheep bent their heads down to the ground so as not to hear him. Behind him ran Tumaleh, the leader of the flock. The other sheep followed her. Caruso brought up the rear, singing his famous Italian arias at the top of his voice. Really, it's a shame we weren't there to hear this strange duet.

By now it was dusk, and the good news had spread through the kibbutz.

"They're coming!"

"And the sheep are with them!"

Young and old ran out from every house and made for the kibbutz gate. The members gathered on both sides of the path and joyfully accompanied the thief-catchers on their way. The sheep were shut into their fold and treated to a big double portion of sweet-smelling hay. Then the two were surrounded while they related over and over again all that had happened on that great day. When darkness fell the adults returned home, but the youngsters crowded into the tattered watchmen's tent to drink coffee and listen to stories until late into the night.

On the following day the sheikh appeared on his magnificent mare and was served fragrant coffee and tasty candy. Then the long series of discussions and negotiations began. The sheikh promised to punish his guilty tribesmen and, with his usual cunning, washed his hands of the whole affair. It was quite obvious that the two had done the deed without his knowledge—in fact, he swore it upon oath. Finally, he promised that this would be the last incident of its kind; no longer would any member of his tribe lay hands on anything belonging to the kibbutz, not even a thread or a shoelace.

So peace reigned once again between the two sides, and their friendship continued. Caruso and Shai won respect and esteem in all the black tents of the bedouin in the district, and around the coffee tray they talked of their deeds by the small fires.

2

. . .

The Camel Riders

A caravan of camels advanced up the road. It was led by an old bedouin on a small gray donkey, whose head was bent earthward and who was followed by three camels roped together. The camels carried large baskets filled with *gefet*—the oil-soaked olive pulp left after the oil-pressing—for lighting the baker's oven. The camels loped along awkwardly, wearing their usual disdainful, supercilious expression.

The old bedouin rode sidesaddle, leading the caravan toward the bakery. He halted his mount, hopped down from the saddle, and made the camels kneel down. "Harrrrr . . . harrrrrr . . . harrrrrr," he growled at them gutturally, beating their forelegs with a stick. The camels grumbled and complained to the world at large and showed their large, yellow teeth; but they bent their front knees and finally their hind knees. Eventually they knelt down, keeping their heads held regally erect all the while.

The bedouin entered the bakery and greeted Leibl, the baker. Leibl was an old man whose long beard was kept tucked into his cummerbund as he kneaded the dough and slapped it into round loaves. The pair began to unload the beasts and pour out the contents of the baskets onto the heap of *gefet* by the bakehouse, where Leibl could help himself as he needed it for lighting his oven.

The bedouin was a small, withered, sinewy, agile individual whose face was weathered by the desert sun and wind. His eyes were bright and sharp. He worked quickly, unloading and tipping, and lashing out at a particularly stubborn animal, which retaliated by showing its teeth with rage. He loosened the girth of the saddle and wiped his sweating face on the hem of his cloak. While he worked, he gabbled away incessantly to Leibl in Arabic, though Leibl understood not a single word of that language. Finally, the job was done, and the bedouin went into the bakery to taste Leibl's wares.

While the Arab and baker were occupied in

the bakery, we three stood outside watching the camels. There was Yitzhak, the practical joker, Yirmi, and I. Naturally, it was Yitzhak who called us over to look at the camels. While we were inspecting them, he suggested, "Come on, let's ride the camels!"

"What, without asking?" said Yirmi.

"Of course, without asking," answered Yitzhak. "Why, did you think the bedouin would let us ride his precious camels?"

"O.K.," agreed Yirmi.

"We could have a terrific ride," I contributed.

The three hump-backed creatures lay rhythmically chewing their cud. They stared at us with moist eyes. Yitzhak didn't waste any time. He went over to the donkey and unhitched it from the camels. Then he mounted the leading camel. Yirmi followed suit, mounting the second beast, and I mounted the third.

A camel saddle is made of two wooden poles, one on each side of the hump, linked together with ropes and straps. The camel's head loomed above me with its small ears and two colored tassels, one on each side of its head, decorating the bridle. It was a little frightening to be sitting on such an enormous creature, opening its wide jaws, when you didn't know what it might do next.

Yitzhak shouted, grunted like a camel, and

tried to make his mount rise. But the beast refused to get up. It lay sprawled out, quite indifferent, and continued its rhythmic chewing. Yitzhak beat the camel's neck with a stick, but still it would not rise to its feet. Finally, he grew angry and began shouting, grunting, and beating; at last the camel stirred its hind legs and began to stand up. I saw Yitzhak drop his stick with fright and grab the two poles of the saddle. His camel was roped to the second camel, which also began to rise. Yirmi let out a surprised yell.

Suddenly, I felt the saddle rock under me, and I was thrown forward as my camel raised its hind legs. I gripped the saddle, and while I was still rocking and swaying the beast raised its forelegs. I was carried aloft, holding fast to the saddle and feeling my face grow greener. The three of us were now camel-riding.

"Wonderful!" shouted Yitzhak.

"Ye-e-e-s . . . er . . . won-n-n-der . . . f-ful," stammered Yirmi.

"Lovely," I called, and looked down from my great height at the ground, which for some reason seemed to be an awfully long way off.

Yitzhak's camel began to make its way down the winding path between the olive groves.

"It's marvelous riding a camel, isn't it?" cried Yitzhak cheerfully.

"Yes!" I agreed, swaying back and forth,

back and forth, on the camel's back until I felt my insides turn over.

"It's a bit difficult," volunteered Yirmi.

"Oh, what do you know about it?" grumbled Yitzhak scornfully.

"Yes, what do you know about it?" I echoed, and felt the pain in my muscles where my legs gripped and rubbed against the bony, hairy hump.

Yitzhak lifted one leg over the camel's neck and seated himself sidesaddle, in the correct position. We copied him and immediately felt more comfortable. The caravan progressed through the olive grove and moved along the path leading through the fields.

The beasts moved serenely, arching their necks proudly and plodding along the hill on their wide hooves. It was hot. The saddle creaked as the camels plodded along the path.

We had crossed the wheatfields, and the camels continued on toward the distant horizon.

"Where are they going?" I shouted to Yitzhak.

"Straight on," he answered.

"Yes, I can see that," I shouted back. "But straight on to where?"

"Per-perhaps we could turn back?" stammered Yirmi.

"I think we'd better go back soon," I called. "We've ridden far enough."

"Yes, I agree," answered Yitzhak. "But how on earth do we turn the camels around?"

He tried pulling the reins to the right and to the left, but his beast ignored this and continued straight on along the path, with the other two camels following.

"Well, what's happening?" asked Yirmi.

"The camel doesn't want to turn around," Yitzhak called back.

"What shall we do?" cried Yirmi fearfully.

"The devil knows," moaned Yitzhak.

The three camels plodded onward, carrying the three of us with them.

"Turn right, right turn!" shouted Yitzhak, but in vain, for his camel trod on relentlessly, as if the command had not been directed at it at all.

"It won't take any notice," I shouted to Yitzhak. "It's used to being given commands in Arabic."

"That's true," replied Yitzhak. "But I don't know what to say to camels in Arabic."

"What are we going to do?" repeated Yirmi.

We were complete novices at riding these huge creatures, and they were plodding ceaselessly ahead, taking no notice of us whatsoever. We rode and rode; we thought we would have to ride right into the bedouin encampment. The bedouins would be very surprised to see the three camels minus the donkey and the old bedouin. Who knows what they might do to us. We ought to stop—but how?

The three camels continued serenely on their way, and it seemed as though we could never stop them, that they would plod onward like this until the Day of Judgment. Our backsides were sore from rubbing against the poles of the saddle and the hump. Our backs ached from the shaking and swaying. The sun was hot, and our perspiration streamed down, making us feel very uncomfortable; our bare skin was sunburnt. Yet the camels continued farther and farther along the path. It seemed as if no power on earth could stop the three hump-backed beasts with their heads held high, their tall, rounded humps, their short tails and hard saddles.

Then, just as we were certain that there was no way out of our predicament, that our fate had been sealed and that there was nothing we could do about it, just as despair gnawed at our hearts and every cheerful thought was pushed away into a corner of our minds—at that very moment, Yitzhak slipped from the saddle. He clung for a second to the camel's neck, then slid down its foreleg and fell to the ground. He rose, dirty and dusty, and ran behind his beast to grab the rope hanging from the bridle.

"You nasty camel!" shouted Yitzhak angrily and dragged at the rope. "You silly hump!" he yelled and yanked the rope to the right. The camel's neck was pulled in that direction, and the beast began to turn to the right, with the other two camels following suit. Yitzhak dragged his camel after him, and we followed. He began to walk back down the path, leading the camels, just like the bedouin's little donkey.

"Wonderful!" called Yirmi.

"Terrific!" I shouted.

"Wonderful, wonderful," muttered Yitzhak. "You're sitting pretty up there, but I have to do the walking!"

We made no reply, though I would have changed places with him happily and swapped my uncomfortable perch for the opportunity of stretching my legs. But I knew it was difficult to slide off the camel's back, so I thought I'd better say nothing.

At midday a strange procession entered the Jewish settlement. It was led by Yitzhak, who was covered with dust and crimson with rage. He held a rope tied to a riderless camel. Behind it came two camels carrying riders with sore backsides and chafed skin, their bones aching and creaking.

At the bakery the bedouin was making quite a fuss. He was shouting that his camels had suddenly vanished into thin air. A crowd had gathered at the sound of his complaints. Advice was proffered freely. Someone argued that it was impossible. Someone else cried angrily, "Lawlessness!" A third protested, "How could three camels suddenly disappear just like that, in broad daylight, as if the earth had swallowed them up?" A fourth embarked on a long anecdote. At that moment, our caravan appeared.

The bedouin let out a yell of joy and rushed over to his camels, murmuring guttural endearments to them. He grabbed the rope from Yitzhak and grunted and shouted; the camels, with magnificent indifference, folded their legs beneath them and lay down.

While the bedouin rushed about tending his beloved camels, muttering sweet nothings to them, we were surrounded by the crowd. Some people shouted, "Rascals!" Others protested, "What nerve!" A few merely folded their arms and directed angry glances at us. We dismounted and stretched our aching bones and muscles. It was good to stand on terra firma again, after pitching and rolling on the "ship of the desert" as if it were a ship on the high seas. Then we looked at each other and broke into loud, hearty laughter. It was good to laugh and laugh, a pleasure to feel the ground under our feet. People around us looked at us with astonishment, as if to say, "What on earth is there to laugh at?"

Still we continued to roar with laughter, and Yitzhak shouted, "What a funny ride!"

Yirmi agreed. "Yes, very funny indeed."

"Yes, it was funny, but I'm glad it's over," I contributed.

Then the bedouin made his camels stand up. He mounted his donkey, and the caravan moved off out of our settlement, rocking and swaying, until it disappeared around a bend in the road.

3

. . .

A Good Shot

Late one evening we heard five loud reports in the east. We were sitting on our porch, drinking an evening glass of tea. My father cocked his ears at the sound of the gunfire, which echoed loudly in the surrounding nocturnal silence.

"What can it be?" he asked anxiously.

He rose and peered through the thick darkness. The rest of us remained silent. There was an oppressive feeling in the air, as if something terrible was about to happen, something we had to sit and wait for, powerless to do anything about it.

While we sat in silence, we heard the sound of running footsteps on the cobblestones. Suddenly, Mr. Kalabriski burst into the pool of light shed by the porch lamp, clutching his rifle, which was of the type known as *abu hamsa*—Arabic for "father of five"—because its chamber held five bullets.

"I got them!" he shouted triumphantly while he was still quite a way off, brandishing his rifle victoriously. "I'm sure I've killed them, the wretches. Ah, that was a really good shot!"

He slowed down his pace and walked sedately up the path toward the porch, his long black shadow trailing behind him on the white gravel. He wore a victorious grin on his large face. His clothes were dusty and his shoes muddy.

"I lay in wait and shot five bullets at them," he crowed. "Now they'll know who they are dealing with. No one treats me like that and gets away with it."

"Who did you shoot?" asked my father in alarm.

"The raiders."

"Which raiders?"

"The ones who came to eat the beets from my beet field."

"Do you know who they were?"

"Yes, of course—wild boars. They came and chewed up my beets and thought they could fill their bellies to their hearts' content and get off scot-free. But they were wrong! No one steals my beets whenever he likes. I've got a good rifle, and what's more, I know how to use it."

We didn't say a word. I heard my mother's breathing grow quieter and my father's sigh of relief.

"Tomorrow, I'm going over there with the wagon to bring back the two boars. There was a small one and a big one, probably a sow and one of its young. I heard them chewing my beets and shot them at close range. They say a full-grown boar has a hundred *rotels* of good flesh on it. Of course," he said with a wink, "not a word to Yochai, the ritual slaughterer. He thinks pig's meat is the most terrible abomination!"

Mr. Kalabriski then made off in the direction of his house, still clutching his rifle, with the air of one who is pleased with himself and his day's work.

The wild boar episode had begun that morning. Kalabriski's beet field adjoins Ben-Porat's. That morning Ben-Porat had come down to his field and found it covered with big pieces of juicy red beetroot. The animal that had been eating the beets had rooted them out with its tusks, and had trampled and crushed whole rows of beet plants with its trotters. I was nearby hoeing our tomato patch at the time, and I saw Ben-Porat rushing this way and that in despair, running his hands through the sparse gray hairs that barely covered his scalp, in a gesture of desperation and misery.

Meanwhile, Kalabriski had rolled up in his wagon to work in his field, proudly driving his gray horse. He wore a broad-brimmed straw hat and knee boots. He had come to irrigate his beet field and had brought a spade with him. Kalabriski reined in his horse at Ben-Porat's field, jumped down from the wagon, and marched complacently into the field.

"Good morning, Mr. Ben-Porat."

"Huh, what do you mean, good morning? It's anything but a good morning. It's a plague of locusts. It's leprosy, but not a good morning!"

"What's happened here, Mr. Ben-Porat?"

"They've destroyed half my beet patch, half the patch! May a terrible plague fall upon their mothers, the gangsters. May they perish horribly!"

"Who did it?" Kalabriski walked into the field and bent down to examine the soil. "It was wild boars," he concluded.

"Those accursed animals," railed Ben-Porat. "Last week they dug up Minkowsky's whole turnip field, and three days ago they destroyed Segal's cabbages. Only yesterday, they chewed up Goldberg's lettuce, damn them!"

"Wild boars are dangerous raiders," agreed Kalabriski, and glanced toward at his own beet field.

"You wait until they pay you a visit," warned Ben-Porat.

"Thanks very much," replied Kalabriski. "That's a pleasure I could do without!"

"No, no, I don't wish such a plague on you, heaven forbid," Ben-Porat hurriedly reassured him. "But who can guarantee that they won't come and root about in your field?"

"My field? Ho, ho, if they do, they'll get a warm welcome!"

"What do you mean?"

"Wait and see," replied Kalabriski mysteriously.

He returned to his wagon and drove off to his own field.

That evening Kalabriski oiled his rifle and loaded it with five bullets. When darkness fell, he left home and went off to his beet field. A gentle westerly breeze was blowing. Kalabriski positioned himself at the eastern edge of the field so that the boars would not pick up his scent.

He lay in wait for many hours, his rifle at the ready, to ambush the raiders. He had the patience of a true hunter and did not close an eyelid, although he was tired after a long day's work.

About midnight he heard someone moving in the field. He immediately stretched out flat and cocked his rifle. There was someone in his field. He heard the sound of chewing and the rustle of plants being crushed. Kalabriski was almost beside himself with rage, but calmed himself down by imagining how he would greet the raiders with a hail of bullets and put an end to their activities forever.

The sound of chewing grew louder. Two dark silhouettes were discernible against the paler background of the sky. One was large and one small. The pair approached, munching ceaselessly. When they were very close to him, Kalabriski aimed his rifle at the larger shape and fired. He was so close to his quarry, he did not even need to use the rifle sights.

There was a muffled snort and a strangled cry, and the creature fell down. Kalabriski cocked his rifle again and aimed at the smaller shape. Just to make sure, he fired remaining three bullets at the figures, emptying the magazine. He had no flashlight with him, so he shouldered his rifle and ran triumphantly back to the village to spread the good news that the raiders were dead. Wild boars would never visit the allotments again.

Next day Kalabriski hitched his horse to his biggest wagon. He asked my father and me to accompany him and help him load the wild boars onto the cart. "They must be very heavy," he told us. "One of them was positively enormous!"

We agreed to go with him. He put a large coil of strong, thick rope into the wagon, hoisted himself onto the box, and cracked the whip over the gray, which trotted off toward the fields. We sat in the back.

As we approached the field, Kalabriski reminded us of his presence by shouting triumphantly, "Look, over there. There are the two boars! What did I tell you? I'm a good shot, aren't I?"

Two dark shapes were discernible amid the green of the field.

"Are wild boars black?" queried my father, doubtfully.

"Well, these are very dark," replied Kalabriski.

My father shrugged, but said nothing.

The wagon halted by the field. Kalabriski took the coils of rope with him, and we followed him into the field, which showed unmistakable traces of the raiders who had chewed up his beets.

"Careful, don't tread on my beets," Kalabriski warned us. He cultivated his crops with ardent devotion and protected them fiercely. Even now he remembered to take care of what was left of the beets, though the field was covered with chewed bits of beetroot.

We approached the bodies, with Kalabriski in the lead. We reached the scene of the crime. Lying in a large pool of congealed blood was Kalabriski's best cow. A large hole gaped in her stomach. A long cord, frayed at one end, was tied around her

neck. Nearby lay a small calf, a bullet hole in its head.

"Oh, no, what have I done?" cried Kalabriski in horror. "The cow was tied up in the clover field so that she could eat at night."

"She seems to have broken her rope," observed my father, "and she got into your beet field instead of the boars."

Kalabriski's face was yellow with misery. He bent over the cow and gazed at her. She was a fine Dutch cow, an excellent milker. Kalabriski mumbled something. I drew near and heard him saying, "A good shot, eh? Such a good shot . . . O Lord!"

4

. . .

The Red *Djinn*

"Without a camel there is no life—and without a mare there is no honor."—Bedouin proverb

Jamila was the name of the roan mare belonging to Shimshi, the field watchman. She was a fine thoroughbred, a queen among horses, beautiful and aristocratic. Her russet coat gleamed, her legs were slender and muscular, her flanks broad, and her back slightly concave, an indication of great strength. Her neck arched proudly, her head was small, and her eyes were bright and intelligent.

With her ears sharply pricked in awareness and her thick tail held high, she moved lightly and gracefully. All her qualities illustrated the Arab saying "There is no mare superior to a roan." She was a unique animal.

Jamila had been bought from a bedouin sheikh who was impoverished; otherwise he would never have sold her. The sale was only partial, as is customary in horse trading. Her first two fillies were to go to her previous owner. Another condition laid down by the sheikh when he sold the mare to Shimshi was that she should never be harnessed to a wagon or a plough like an ordinary workhorse. This fine thoroughbred mare was for riding only.

Shimshi bedecked Jamila with fringes, tassels, and embroidered saddlebags and girth. He looked very fine seated in the saddle, as she pranced along gracefully—it made one green with envy. Jamila means "beautiful" in Arabic. It would have been hard to find a more suitable name for the mare than Jamila, with the gay sound of the *J*, the soft *mi*, and the short, sharp ending *la:* Ja-mi-la.

One day Abu Yussuf, the sheikh of the Arab-el-Haybe tribe, invited Shimshi to visit his tent. The Arab-el-Haybe was a large bedouin tribe, and their sheikh was aggressive, cunning, ferocious, and cruel. Shimshi mounted Jamila and set off for the tribe's encampment.

He was greeted by a pack of mangy, bedraggled-looking dogs. These were bedouin dogs, whose ears are sharp and whose bark is loud so that everyone knows immediately when they have spotted a wayfarer approaching the tents. The sheikh's son peeped out of his father's tent and disappeared again immediately. Then the sheikh himself came out to greet Shimshi. His appearance was impressive. He had a short, full beard shot through with gray, and wore a long striped cloak with an embroidered hem. A Mauser pistol and a curved silver dagger were stuck in his belt.

Shimshi dismounted, and the sheikh's son came to lead the mare away to be fed and watered and to loosen her girth. "*Tfadal*—please come in,"

the sheikh invited. The pair removed their shoes and stepped onto the carpeted floor of the tent.

Abu Yussuf began to prepare the coffee in a sooty, copper pot with a long curved spout called a *bakaratch*. First he ground the coffee beans in a wooden mortar pitted with tiny dents; then he poured the coffee grounds into the pot. He added water and set the pot on the embers of the fire which was always kept burning in the middle of the tent. The Arabs say, "Coffee should be black as night, hot as Hell, strong as love, and bitter as death." The sheikh's coffee fulfilled these requirements adequately. It was fragrant and burning hot, and was drunk from tiny cups without handles. The guest blew gently over the surface of the brew to cool it, and drank it down noisily to show his host what a delicious drink he had prepared.

After the pair had sipped coffee for a while, the host opened the conversation. "Listen to me, Shimshi."

"I am listening, honored sheikh."

"I have something to say to you."

"Speak. I am at your service."

"Behold. Allah has given you a beautiful mare."

"There is none better than my Jamila."

"Now, you must know that my soul hungers for your mare. She shall be mine!"

"How could I part from my Jamila?"

"I know, she is a wonderful mare—more precious than a wife or a daughter. Yet I shall weigh out much silver into your palm in return for her, and her first filly shall be yours. There—the matter is settled. The mare shall become my possession."

"Sheikh, I know you are most generous; yet I cannot be parted from my mare. She is most dear to me. Her price is above silver."

"That is unfortunate, my dear guest. Yet I am unable to renounce my desires. Jamila shall be mine."

"I have finished my drink," replied Shimshi, rising to his feet. "The time has come for me to take my leave."

"I know many men," warned the sheikh, "who have crossed Sheikh Abu Yussuf. Their fate is known only to the vulture in the skies and to the jackal in the fields."

"Good-bye, kind host. Thank you for the coffee."

The host accompanied his guest to his mare and helped him to mount by holding the saddle. Hospitality is one thing, discord and disputes are another, and sacred traditions may not be broken lightly.

"Good-bye, sheikh."

"Good-bye, good-bye. You have heard what I have to say."

"I have heard."

"Salaam aleikum."

"Aleikum salaam."

Shimshi rode off on Jamila, deep in thought. It would be extremely unpleasant to have to clash with the powerful sheikh, who had many tribesmen and would not hesitate to send them to ambush a rival or plunge a dagger into his heart. It would also be most unwise to disturb the peace in the area, just for the sake of a mare. Bedouins are bound by the *gom*, or blood vengeance, and each shot fired could bring endless acts of revenge in its wake.

As Shimshi rode along pondering his fate and that of Jamila, he spotted old Ali coming toward him on his donkey. Ali was an elder from the Arab village near the Jewish settlement, a man famous for his cunning and sharp wit. His face was old and wrinkled, but his eyes twinkled and sparkled with intelligence. The pair met in the middle of the road. It is customary for the horseman to greet the donkey-rider first.

"Marhaba," Shimshi hailed Ali.

"Marhabtein," replied Ali.

The two riders dismounted and went to sit in the shade of an olive tree to rest for a moment and enjoy a friendly chat.

"You look sad," began Ali.

"Yes," sighed Shimshi. "Unfortunately, I am in serious trouble."

" 'He who is mournful in trouble increases

his troubles tenfold,' " quoted Ali. "Tell me your troubles and lighten your heart," he urged.

Shimshi told the whole story of the sheikh's unreasonable demand for Jamila, his beloved mare, his best friend, from whom he could never be parted. How could he hand her over to the sheikh?

Ali sat for a while, deep in thought. Finally he announced, "I swear upon my own self and upon my neck that I shall arrange the whole matter—and it will not end in battle."

"How?" asked Shimshi.

"There is no God but Allah, and Mohammed is His Prophet," replied Ali. "The All-merciful will send wisdom into my heart."

"I sincerely hope so. If you succeed, Ali, then I promise you shall have a new cloak, a new pair of shoes, a new *keffiyeh*, a good *rotel* of coffee, and two *rotels* of sugar."

The two parted, each going his separate way.

Ali rode off to Sheikh Abu Yussuf's tent. He was taken into the tent and offered hospitality. Having drunk the bedouin coffee and smoked a *nargileh*, an Arabic water pipe, the sheikh and Ali embarked upon a long conversation ranging over such subjects as the welfare of the sheikh's family, the state of his flocks, the weapons most worth having, the sheikh's children, and so on. Finally the conversation came around to the subject of mares, a familiar and well-loved topic in bedouin tents.

"While on the subject of mares, O great and powerful sheikh," said Ali, "I have a strange and amazing story to tell you."

Now, the Arabs believe that a thoroughbred horse has occult powers and can bring its owner good or bad luck.

"Behold, O sheikh," Ali began, "yesterday I was riding toward the Jewish settlement when a riderless mare cantered toward me . . ."

"Riderless?"

"Yes! She was quite alone. As she came near, I recognized her as Jamila, the roan belonging to the Jew."

"Jamila?"

"Yes, O sheikh, Jamila. The mare came up to me and stopped. 'She must have run away,' I thought. 'How could she gallop off without her rider?' "

"Indeed, it is most strange," murmured the sheikh. "Alone! She's been broken in. She would not run away if she was let loose."

"True, O sheikh. But the story is not ended. The mare suddenly opened her mouth and said, in human language, 'Peace be with you!' "

"Allah Akbar!" exclaimed the sheikh in fright. "Most great God, the horse spoke to you?"

"Yes, O sheikh, she spoke to me. I quickly whispered the name of Allah, so that she might at least leave me alive. But she continued. 'Are

you Ali, the son of Hussein, the father of Kamal?' "

"The mare knew your name, and the name
of your father, and the name of your eldest son?"

"Yes, O sheikh, she knew. I was so frightened, I fell off my donkey. I covered my face with
my *keffiyeh* and lay where I had fallen. A *djinn*, a
demon, must dwell in her."

"If a *djinn* attacks a mare and enters her
body, terrible things can happen," mused the
sheikh.

"Well, dear sheikh, I lay there for a while,"
continued Ali. "Then I lifted my *keffiyeh* and peeped
out—and the mare had gone! 'Perhaps I dreamed it
all,' I thought to myself. But no; there were the
hoofprints on the road."

"May the name of Allah be praised," muttered the sheikh in a daze. "It is good that He called
you here this day. The roan mare is surely a *djinn*
and not a real mare."

"Yes, sheikh, she is a demon, a terrible, awful
demon. Only the *Yahud*, the Jews, can rule such evil
spirits."

The sheikh's face was deathly pale. "I was
about to buy the mare from the watchman. She
would have brought bad luck to me and my tribe."
Then he told Ali about Shimshi's visit.

"Keep your soul safe from harm," counseled
Ali sagely. "He who values his soul should keep his

distance from this mare. There are mares who are bad luck and bring only misfortune and harm to their owners."

The next day the sheikh's son rode up to Shimshi's house.

"The sheikh has sent me to tell you that he no longer wants your mare," he told Shimshi. "He does not want Jamila. He sends greetings to Shimshi, who will always be a welcome guest in the tents of the Arab-el-Haybe."

So Ali got his new cloak, his shoes, and his *keffiyeh*, plus two *rotels* of coffee and four *rotels* of sugar, for good measure. And from then on, Jamila was known to the Arabs as "the Red *Djinn*."

5

. . .

Prickly Pears

When the season for the summer fruits—
grapes, plums, peaches, melons, and watermelons—
has finally ended, and only purple, soft, overripe
figs remain here and there among their distinctive
leaves, which are shaped like the outspread fingers
of a hand, then the prickly pear comes into its own.
This cactus fruit has many virtues. It is to be found
in plentiful supply for anyone who wants it. It
grows on the cactus plant, whose fat, fleshy leaves
are covered with sharp spines. Anyone fancying the

pink and yellow fruit can pluck it from the top of a leaf and eat his fill.

The prickly pear ripens when all the other summer fruits have ended their season, and the summer is almost over—when the weather is stifling and sultry, the fields are covered with parched yellow stubble, and swirls of dust rise from them, blown about by hot gusts of wind. In the middle of a heat wave you can peel off the prickly outer skin of the fruit, revealing the glistening interior, and sink your teeth into the cool, orange-colored flesh, swallow the seeds, and taste the refreshing sweet flavor. In hot weather the prickly pear is a dish fit for a king.

The Arabs call the prickly pear *sabres*. In Hebrew it is called *tzabar*. The Arabs sell the fruit from their donkeys. They load the animals with two baskets filled to the brim with the choicest specimens, and use a simple scale—made of a wooden yoke to which two tin bowls are tied with string—to weigh them out. The weights are stones. The Arabs drive their beasts through the Jewish villages crying, "*Sabres, sabres, tayib sabres!*" These are the professional *sabres*-sellers. There are also Arab peasants who are in the habit of trying to sell anything with a conceivable market value to the Jewish villages in their spare time. When the reaping is over, the wheat flailed, and the grain stored, there is time to while away the hours bargaining until the first rains fall and the ploughing season begins.

The thorny cactus plant that bears the prickly pear is used as a fence and a boundary marker between fields and plots of land. It thus has a dual purpose—it bears a refreshing fruit and serves as a fence which costs nothing to erect. The plant is propagated very simply. When the leaves are scattered over the ground, they take root, growing tall, fat leaves covered with huge spikes like a thorny crown. The fruit and leaves also disseminate the plants by means of the minute prickles, which are carried away by the wind and stick to flesh and clothing, burning and irritating the skin.

The only creature capable of eating cactus leaves is the camel. Its horny lips and tongue are impervious to the needle-sharp spines. The camel stretches its long neck upward to get at the topmost, juiciest leaves, which it chews heartily, a greenish saliva dripping from the corners of its mouth. I have often enviously watched the camel doing this. It makes your mouth water and almost makes you long to taste the fat, fleshy leaves.

Yet I have seen this cactus serve a very different purpose. This is how it happened.

I have already told you about Jamila, the roan mare owned by Shimshi, the field watchman. The story I am about to tell you concerns her. She was the best-broken and the best-bred mare I have ever come across, and that is saying a great deal. In the days I'm writing about, every sheikh and every notable had a beautiful thoroughbred mare, and the wealthier and more eminent the man, the better his mare. Some knew the genealogy of their mares. They compiled a family tree, called a *hijajeh*, which might show her ancestors right back to the offspring of Mohammed's own mare.

The bedouins are sometimes more attached to their mares than they are to their wives and daughters. If a mare dies, the bedouin will mourn and say sadly, "She was like a son (or a daughter) to me, and I grieve for her as I would for one of my own children."

The bedouins, who dwell in "houses of hair," as they call their goat-hair or camel-hair tents, enjoy telling long yarns about the legendary feats of famous mares and their riders. When such tales were told, Jamila's name was always mentioned. She had become a legend in her own lifetime. After the Arabs had begun to call her "the Red *Djinn*," even more tales and legends sprang up around her. Shimshi never bothered to refute or repudiate the halo of glory surrounding his mare. The greater the horse's reputation, the greater is that of its owner; and one of a good watchman's assets is his reputation. As the proverb says, "A good name is better than good oil." Sometimes it is enough for thieves to know that there is a brave and fearless watchman in the vicinity to deter them from stealing in that particular area.

Shimshi's horse was also the heroine of many *mayadin*. The Arabs call their horse races *maidan*, which actually means the large arena in which the races take place. Tent-dwellers and villagers gather regularly to watch a big *maidan* and see the riders perform feats. This usually takes place on an anniversary or a religious festival, or during a *fantasia* or wedding.

Shimshi was devoted to his mare and tended her with lavish care. He would feed her lumps of sugar from his hand, select the choicest foliage for her, cutting it himself, and find her the best grains of barley. He would give her carobs (a kind of local fruit) to crunch, and let her eat her fill so that she would grow stronger.

Shimshi lived right at the end of the settlement in a little house of black chiseled basalt blocks. The stable, which was next to the house, held Jamila and her riding tackle, the saddle, *huraj* (embroidered saddlebags), bridle, bit, and other pieces of equipment. Surprisingly enough, Shimshi never locked the stable door, even on dark winter nights when thieves and robbers are often about, pitch darkness being best suited to their nefarious purposes. The reason he didn't was simple.

Jamila possessed a quality rare among mares,

one found commonly only among the finest thoroughbreds. She would allow no one to mount her except her master, Shimshi. She obeyed him like a trained dog. He could leave her loose in a field, and she would not move from the spot until she heard her master whistle to her. It was said that some of the most accomplished riders had tried their skill on her, but they had always ended up on the ground with broken bones. The moment Jamila felt the weight of a rider on her back, she would run wild, kicking up her hind legs and leaping about— never stopping until the unlucky rider was thrown from the saddle. She thus gained a formidable reputation, and no one dared go near her.

One person decided to ride her come what may: my friend Yitzhak. Yitzhak was one of the best riders in the settlement and an expert in the ways of horses. Some people are born with an instinctive understanding of animals and know them and can handle them better than others. Such a person was Yitzhak. When a wild horse or an unruly colt had to be broken in, they called Yitzhak. He had a firm, steady hand with horses. He would talk to them gently, coax, comfort, and stroke them and would usually manage to get his way with them.

One day Shimshi left his horse by the threshing floor while he went to see if any grain had been stolen from the heaps left there overnight. Yitzhak and I happened by. "Look, here's the roan mare," Yitzhak said to me as we stood outside the barn. "Shimshi has left her here."

"Well, so what?"

"I want to try to ride her, and this is a marvelous opportunity."

"It isn't worth it; you know how she runs wild."

"It's no good. I've made up my mind. I'll ride her. She's a marvelous beast for a clash of wills, and she has a strong temperament."

"Temperament? A horse?"

"Yes, a horse with temperament. Animals have characters just like human beings. Some are honest, others are cunning. Some are cowardly, some stupid, and so on. Only thing is that their characters are not obvious as people's are. Jamila is a beast with temperament and a sense of honor and dignity. She is a wonderful mare, I'm telling you."

"It isn't worth the risk."

Yitzhak made no reply. He approached the mare. She stood beneath a eucalyptus tree, peacefully munching the greenery growing there. Yitzhak moved close to her and laid a hand on her neck, which was decorated with trappings. A shiver ran through her glistening tawny frame, but she remained standing where she was.

Yitzhak stroked the nape of her neck and tickled her under the jawbone, a trick horses love. She pricked up her small ears and lifted her head. She still stood calmly, only her tail arched slightly. Yitzhak put his hand on the saddle and pressed down, then lifted it up again so that the mare would gradually become used to the weight of a rider. Finally, he put his left hand on the saddle pommel and leapt lightly into the saddle. He thrust his feet into the stirrups and took hold of the reins, hugging the mare's body with his thighs and knees. He shortened and tightened the reins so that the bit would press against her mouth.

The roan stood quite still. For a moment I thought that Yitzhak would succeed in riding her. In the past all the would-be riders had tried to jump straight into the saddle. Only Yitzhak had begun by coaxing the mare first. She had always started her tricks the moment a rider so much as touched her. Apparently this time she had sensed, with the instinct of an intelligent animal, that this was no ordinary rider.

Yitzhak clicked his tongue to make Jamila move, but she remained stationary. He dug his heels into her flanks. Suddenly, Jamila leapt into the air, kicked out with her hind legs, sprang forward onto her forelegs, arched and straightened her back, and hurled her rider about. Yitzhak clung tenaciously to the saddle and bent her neck downward. She danced like a whirling dervish. The dust rose in clouds. Her hide glistened with sweat. All that could be seen of her were flashing hooves, a flying tail, a swirling mane, and a head that moved this way and that, while the rider's body, rocking and swaying, could occasionally be seen in the midst of this frightful frenzy.

The roan mare did not manage to throw Yitzhak, so she broke into a furious gallop, flying off out of sight behind the barn.

"Who's that?" asked Shimshi when he came back to fetch Jamila.

"It's Yitzhak. He's made up his mind to ride your mare."

"Aha . . ."

Shimshi was unperturbed. He was used to people trying their hand at riding Jamila.

"Do you think he's managed it?"

"I shouldn't think so."

"But he's kept his seat so far."

"Yes, but wait and see."

Around us all was peace and tranquillity, compared to the furious storm that had surrounded us only a moment previously. A column of dust was discernible in the distance. The column grew bigger and a russet figure broke through it, rushing headlong toward us. It was the roan mare, carrying a crouching rider, Yitzhak. Jamila had not managed to throw him.

The mare was a beautiful sight. Her tail streamed back, her head was stretched forward, her belly was taut and low to the ground, and her hooves flashed and twinkled. Her long mane flew in the wind. A whitish foam flecked her mouth, and the sweat glistened on her red flanks.

She reached the eucalyptus tree and began to gallop round it. She bucked and threw her hind legs high into the air, but could not throw her rider. Suddenly, she broke off and cantered beneath the overhanging branches of the tree. Yitzhak clung to her back, digging his knees into her flanks. I saw her pass under the stout green branches. I saw them flailing her rider. For a second it seemed as though Yitzhak would fall. But no, he still held on.

"He'll make her surrender," I told Shimshi.

"This is the first time anyone has managed to stay on her so long," he admitted.

The mare galloped around in a circle, but suddenly she changed direction and made full tilt for the nearby orchard, which was fenced off with prickly pear cactus. The mare rushed up to the fence without slowing down. There was a narrow opening in the middle of the fence, between two large cacti. She broke through the gap, her red body highlighted against the rich green background of

the plants. On her back lay a black blob, her rider.
With a fearsome leap, her red body passed between
the prickly pear plants, actually brushing close to
them. Then the black shape was seen to roll off her
and was thrown among the cacti. Shimshi gave me
an I-told-you-so look.

We both rushed over to the cactus fence.
Jamila stood still, her flanks rising and falling with
her heavy breathing, foam bubbling from her
mouth and dripping to the ground. Deep in the
spiny cacti lay Yitzhak, badly cut and scratched. His
whole body was streaked with blood. He had protected his face and eyes with his hands so that they,
at least, had escaped damage.

Shimshi drew his knife and cut away at the
cacti so that we could get to Yitzhak. The huge
spines tore at the skin of our hands. We had to be
careful not to let the tiny powdery prickles touch
the exposed flesh. Even so, a few minute thorns
clung to the broken skin, burning and itching.

Shimshi lay Yitzhak across the mare and led
her to Yitzhak's house. I ran for the doctor. He
tended Yitzhak for many hours, drawing the thorns
out with tweezers, then bandaging the wounds
after pouring a large quantity of iodine into
them.

We left Yitzhak lying in his house and went
off. I gave the roan mare a look of hatred. "You

wicked beast, look what you've done to Yitzhak! Tfoo!" I spat at her, "cursed be the name of 'the Red *Djinn.*'" I looked away to avoid seeing her—just in time to intercept Shimshi's glance of pride at her.

6

. . .

Roast Chicken for Dessert

Shlomo of Safad had many nicknames. The Arabs called him "Abu Shaul—father of Saul," after his eldest son. The Jews of upper Galilee called him "the Horseman of Galilee" because for decades he had ridden the roads and paths of Galilee on his thoroughbred mare, decked out in all her trappings. He hunted thieves and cattle and sheep rustlers, restored peace between feuding bedouin tribes, and settled family quarrels. He was like a brother to the most eminent bedouin sheikhs and was a friend and counselor to the *mukhtars* or head-men of the Arab villages.

Shlomo became a legend in his own stormy, eventful lifetime. He was a giant of a man, strongly and heavily built, with powerful, muscular hands. It was said he could pick up a young bullock as easily as if it were a newborn babe. There were also many dubious characters who had felt the weight of his hand—something they were unlikely to forget in a hurry.

For many years Shlomo had lived and worked in Galilee, patrolling on his mare between the Jewish settlements of Rosh Pina to the south and Metulla in the extreme north, at the foot of Mount Hermon. He was as much a part of the local scenery as the mountain ranges, the rocky crevices, and the hidden paths.

Shlomo also had another nickname, the one with which this story is concerned. He was called "the Big Paunch," because of his enormous appetite. There were many stories of his amazing capacity for food and drink, and his huge paunch was compared to a bottomless pit. He himself was no mean cook, and could prepare delicacies which no chef would have been ashamed of.

One day Shlomo was riding along with his friend Yirmi. Yirmi was also a watchman and was as expert as Shlomo in guarding, riding, fighting, shooting, and tracking down thieves and rustlers.

It was early in winter. The sky was blue, and the green wheat fields, stretching into the distance, stirred in the light breeze. Shlomo and Yirmi rode along together at a leisurely pace. They were making for the house of the *mukhtar* of the Arab village of Farem, up in the mountains.

The stone and mud huts of the village clung precariously to the hillside of Mount Canaan, looking like blue, yellow, and pink bricks piled one on top of the other. The roof of one house brushed the doorstep of the next, built farther up the slope. The topmost house was the whitewashed home of the *mukhtar*.

A steep path, winding between fig and almond orchards, clumps of prickly pear, and vineyards, led to the village. The horses ambled slowly along, their riders deep in the sort of conversation which only very close friends or lovers can engage in. They exchanged local gossip and the latest stories being told around the coffeepot in the bedouin tents. They also gave each other tips and hints they had received from their respective informers, for without informers a field watchman cannot carry out his functions efficiently.

Both riders were feeling cheerful, thanks to the warm sun, the cool, fresh air, and the wild flowers which grew by the roadside. The conversation finally got around to the subject of eating and drinking. The pair reminisced about the huge feasts held by important sheikhs and the abundant quantity of roast lamb, boiled rice, fragrant coffee, and sweet watermelons they had consumed. For dessert, there was always a *nargileh* to smoke.

Shlomo slapped his huge paunch and declared, "Well, it wouldn't hurt my stomach to be filled up with food right now. A stomach without food is like a saddle without a horse."

Yirmi smiled but said nothing.

"Upon my life," cried Shlomo. "I swear I could eat a whole sheep!"

"Hey, hey," remonstrated Yirmi. "A whole sheep? Complete?"

"No, not complete. The entrails would have to be removed, and the stomach cavity stuffed with good rice. And of course the animal would have to be sheared and skinned. And I'd want something to wash it down with."

"I'm not so sure you could manage it," said Yirmi, and slapped his mare's rump to make her quicken her pace.

"Oh, no?" cried Shlomo, somewhat offended by Yirmi's scepticism.

Yirmi halted his mount and turned to Shlomo. "Listen here, Abu Shaul. If you can eat a whole sheep all by yourself, without any help, I shall cross your palm with five good, solid English pounds sterling, no less! Five crisp new notes issued by the Anglo-Palestine Bank and bearing the portrait of His Majesty the King."

"It's a deal," shouted Shlomo merrily. "That means I'll profit on both counts—I'll have a nice, fat, tasty, tender sheep to eat and win money too!"

"Look, we'll go to the *mukhtar* now, and ask him to prepare a roast sheep for us. All you have to do is prepare your belly to receive it!"

"My belly is ready and willing!"

The pair reached the village. As they rode in, a horde of ragged, runny-nosed urchins, barefoot and with suppurating eyes, surrounded the mares. A barking dog appeared from somewhere, limping on three legs.

Upon hearing the dog bark, the *mukhtar* himself appeared. He was a man in the prime of life. He had a full black beard and wore an expensive cloak bordered with gold embroidery and elegant red leather shoes. His head was adorned with a golden *keffiyeh*, and the glistening black bands of the *agal* which held it in place were decorated with little woolen tassels.

"*Tfadal.*" He invited his guests into the *madafe*, the village guesthouse, where visitors could stay the night and were entertained and served food and fragrant coffee. "Please enter."

The guests stepped onto the mat which their host had spread before them in the customary manner. They sipped coffee, smoked a *nargileh*, and embarked upon the usual formalities of conversation. The villagers and village elders gradually filled the room. They had come to pass the time in conversation and to learn something of what was happening in the great, wide world which Allah had created, and in which He sees everything that happens, great or small.

When most of the elders had seated themselves in a semicircle around the visitors and the *mukhtar*, Yirmi rose from his seat, silenced the company, and informed them of his bet with Shlomo.

A murmur of astonishment ran through the company. The *mukhtar* agreed to the plan and sent his boy to bring a sheep from the flock.

"But make it one of the fattest and tastiest," Shlomo called after him. "You know old Abu Shaul. If there's one thing he can't stand, it's a mangy sheep whose flesh is leathery and which has more bones than meat."

The *mukhtar* alerted his servants, who lit a fire on which to roast the sheep in a huge pot. They slaughtered and skinned the sheep, disembowelled it, and stuffed the cavity with spiced rice. Then they put the whole carcass into the big pot and added mutton fat and spices. All that was to be done now was to wait until it was cooked.

A delicious aroma rose from the roasting sheep. Shlomo's eyes glittered with impatience.

Those present began to hope for a morsel of meat. They had never yet set eyes on a man capable of eating a whole roast sheep single-handedly.

They sat around and chatted, casting furtive glances at the pot from time to time.

Finally, the sheep was roasted and ready for eating. The *mukhtar's* boy served it up on a large copper tray covered with thin fresh *pitta*. The meat was well browned, and the grains of rice were fat, tender, and crisp.

Shlomo drew his knife and cut a huge slice of meat off the leg. He began to eat, closely watched by the whole company, who secretly hoped he would lose the bet—for that would mean that they would be served with whatever meat remained.

Well, I won't keep you in suspense. It was not long before nothing remained of the sheep but bare bones, without a shred of meat sticking to them. As for Shlomo, his paunch had grown even bigger, and his face streamed with sweat from his exertions. He continued to drink great gulps from the jug of water that had been brought for him, and he picked his teeth to remove shreds of meat that had caught between them.

"Wallah!" gasped the company in amazement, all their hopes dashed to pieces. "Allah has indeed created a huge stomach for Abu Shaul. It is a bottomless pit! He has eaten a whole sheep. No man ever witnessed such a feat!"

The bones were thrown to the dogs. Yirmi rose, took out his wallet, and removed five pound notes, which he handed over, one at a time, to Shlomo.

The assembly witnessed the transaction in awed silence.

Toward evening the pair set off again for Safad. The horses trotted through the narrow alleys of the town, their hooves ringing out on the cobblestones and breaking the silence of the sleepy little town.

They passed Moshe Tzipporah's restaurant. This was a little eating place where the customers could eat their fill of delicious dishes prepared by Tzipporah, Moshe's wife. Tzipporah was a wonderful woman. Her husband had even been named after her, Moshe Tzipporah's, meaning Moshe who belongs to Tzipporah.

Shlomo halted his mare and called, "Hey, Yirmi, stop a minute!"

"What's the matter, Shlomo? Why have you stopped in the middle of the street?"

"Because we're outside Moshe Tzipporah's restaurant."

"Well, so what?"

"Listen, Yirmi," sighed Shlomo. "We've ridden a long way and I'm as hungry as a wolf who hasn't eaten for seven days. I didn't even get any dessert at the *mukhtar's*. Come on, let's go into

Moshe Tzipporah's restaurant and use the five pounds you gave me to buy roast chickens. My stomach is as empty and withered as an unfilled goatskin. If I don't eat, I'll die of starvation. Come on, Yirmi. Tzipporah's roast chickens are worth tasting, and after all, I came by your five pounds honestly, didn't I? Money easily earned is easily spent. Come inside, Yirmi, my stomach cries out for its just deserts—dessert!"

The story of the sheep and the chickens was told in the tents of the bedouins and the houses of the Arab peasants. No one knows who was the first to add the nickname "the Big Paunch" to Shlomo's large collection of nicknames, but then one never knows who is the originator of a nickname.

7

. . .

The Girl, the Donkey,
and the Dog

One of the many nicknames of "the Horseman of Galilee," Shlomo, the field watchman, was *Tum El-Asal*, Arabic for "Mouth of Honey." Shlomo had earned this nickname from the Arabs because of the wonderful tales he told. His lips dripped with honeyed words, and no one could hold an audience spellbound the way he could. Because he knew many parables, riddles, and interesting legends the Arabs called him "Mouth of

Honey," for Orientals love stories, parables, and riddles, and they can sit for hours in their black goat-hair tents listening to a storyteller.

One day Shlomo caught a bedouin of the tribe of Sheikh Abu Omer reaping grain that was not his. The bedouin had sneaked into the field, spread his voluminous cloak on the ground, and cut the ears of wheat with a sharp scythe. Then he had bound the wheat into sheaves and laid them on the cloak.

The Horseman of Galilee leapt onto his mare in a flash and silently rode up on the clandestine reaper. When he saw the thief, he drew his pistol and galloped forward. "You villain!" he shouted in Arabic. "So you'd steal wheat, would you?"

The bedouin, caught red-handed, sprang back brandishing his scythe, a sharp and dangerous weapon. But when he saw Shlomo's pistol barrel pointing at him, he halted. His face turned pale with shame and fear, and the scythe fell from his hand.

Shlomo ordered the Arab to gather up the ears of wheat, wrap them in the cloak, and follow him to the tent of Sheikh Abu Omer. Shlomo was familiar with the ways of the bedouin. If he wanted to preserve the ties of friendship so laboriously and patiently woven between bedouin and Jew, he had better not hand the thief over to the police but should take him instead to the sheikh's tent. Abu

Omer was empowered to punish the thief as he thought fit, though in his heart of hearts he probably approved of the deed. Theft is not considered a crime by the bedouin. However, for the sake of appearances, the eminent sheikh would have to pretend to be a man of peace, a keeper of law and order, and an honest, trustworthy, and upright man who scrupulously kept his tribesmen to the straight and narrow path.

As for Shlomo, this act would win him respect, admiration, and sympathy among the bedouin, and would enhance his reputation in their eyes. "He is one of us," they would say—for they hate policemen and the law and order of civilized societies, preferring the rule of their own laws and time-hallowed customs.

When they reached the encampment of Sheikh Abu Omer, Shlomo dismounted and was received with all due honor, as befits a welcome guest. The sheikh's servant took his mare behind the tents to feed and water her, while the guest was ushered into the main tent, which belonged to the sheikh. When he had removed his shoes and stepped onto the mat laid before him in the customary manner, cushions and rugs were placed beneath him. The fragrant coffee was already steaming on the charcoal fire in the middle of the tent.

Shlomo drank three cups of coffee in the prescribed manner, and then began to tell the eminent sheikh of the purpose of his visit. The sheikh immediately ordered the thief to be brought before him, so that he might question him in the presence of the guest.

The thief was a conceited young bedouin, an idler and a good-for-nothing. He wore a ragged, striped robe, and his feet were bare. His eyes were furtive and cunning, and his hair long and greasy. The bedouins use their hair as towels. After eating their greasy mutton, they wipe their hands on their hair, thus killing two birds with one stone—they both clean their hands and rub grease into their hair, which according to them makes it grow long and healthy.

The sheikh sat before the little fire, and Shlomo reclined on cushions facing him. On either side of them sat the elders and leaders of the tribe. They were in the habit of sitting in the sheikh's tent daily, drinking coffee and engaging in idle conversation.

The sheikh cleared his throat and opened the investigation. Suddenly, to the amazement of Shlomo and the rest of the company, the thief prostrated himself at the feet of the sheikh and poured out a volley of hatred and abuse at Shlomo, yelling and shouting and even squeezing out a tear or two. He railed against the terrible injustice that had been done to him. There he had been, walking along innocently, like the honest fellow he was, without a stain on his character; then the watchman had come along, pounced on him, and dragged him back to the encampment like a thief. What had he done? What crime had he committed? He was an honest man. He had never stolen so much as a single grain of barley!

An angry murmur ran through the assembly. This brash thief had acted with a total disregard for courtesy. He had besmirched the honor of a friend, a guest in the encampment. Furthermore, everyone present was well acquainted with this ne'er-do-well and knew him as a habitual thief. And if this were not enough, the watchman had brought overwhelming proof with him: the cloak stuffed with sheaves of wheat and the scythe with which the deed had been done, the handle of which was carved with the thief's own name!

The angry sheikh ordered the thief to leave the tent and announced in thundering tones that an extremely severe punishment would be meted out to him. Then he begged Shlomo not to be angry and to forgive the insult.

Shlomo smiled beneath his huge moustache.

"By your life, O sheikh, the words of this miserable wretch are as the mere buzzing of flies in my ears," he replied. "He must be one of the descendants of the dog who, when they commit a crime, bark loudly afterward in their brashness and conceit."

"The descendants of the dog?" asked the company.

"Yes," replied Shlomo, "the descendants of the dog. Listen, and I shall tell you how men got their respective natures." He sipped his coffee, drew on a *nargileh* and began his tale.

"In the beginning, the great Allah created the heavens and the earth. Then He created plants and animals. Finally, He created one old man who had three sons, these being the first men. Then God created a donkey, a dog, and a young servant girl, and presented all three to the old man. The old man's eldest son was a shepherd. The middle one was a farmer, and the third, a hunter.

"One day as the old man sat at the entrance to his tent his eldest son, the shepherd, came to him bringing a big cheese and a pitcher of fresh milk.

" 'Peace be with you, father.'

" 'And peace be with you, my son. How are your sheep?'

" 'They are all healthy and fat, thanks be to Allah. Their milk is plentiful and their wool excellent.'

" 'Yes, the blessing of Allah is upon you my son.'

" 'Indeed, father, Allah has not withheld His goodness from me. Yet I am lonely. Give me your servant girl for a wife. She can milk the sheep, make

the cheese, and churn the butter. She can weave cloth from the wool and be the mother of my children. Give me the girl for a wife.'

"The father replied, 'I'll think about it. Come back in a week's time and I shall give you my answer.'

"Just as the eldest son had gone, the second son, the farmer, came to the old man. He kissed his father and presented him with a basketful of fresh vegetables.

" 'How are you, my son?'

" 'Thanks be to Allah, I am well and healthy. I till the soil and bring forth bread from the earth. I have only one request to make. Give me the girl for a wife. She can help me work the land. She can cook my meals, dry vegetables for the winter, and be the mother of my children. A man without a wife is like a plough without soil.'

" 'I shall think about it, my son,' replied the old man. 'Come back in a week's time and I shall give you my answer.'

"The farmer had only just left when the third son, the hunter, came to the tent carrying a fresh chunk of meat from an animal he had killed. The hunter gave the meat to the girl to cook and looked at her longingly.

" 'She's a beautiful girl,' he said to his father.

" 'Yes,' agreed the old man, 'and she is clever and hardworking too.'

"The son sat down by his father and laid his huge bow at his feet. 'How are you, father?'

" 'Thanks be to Allah, I am very well—healthy and happy. How does the hunting go, my son?'

" 'There is much game. Allah's fields contain many wild animals. I lack nothing but a wife. Father, give me the girl for a wife. She can tan the hides and make garments and blankets from them. She can roast and boil the meat so that we can eat our fill, and we can raise children.'

"His father replied, 'Come back in a week's time, my son, and I shall give you my answer.'

"The third son bade his father farewell, and the old man sat in thought. To which of his sons should he give his servant girl for a wife? How could he give her to one and thus discriminate against the other two?

"While he sat in deep thought, the angel of God appeared before him. 'First man, why are you sad? Do you lack for anything?'

"The old man poured out his troubles to the angel. The angel said, 'Do not worry, O beloved of God. I shall turn the dog and the donkey into girls so that you can give each son a wife.'

"The angel turned the dog and the donkey into girls, and fashioned them in the likeness of the first girl. The three resembled each other so closely you could not tell them apart.

"A week later the three sons returned. Their father gave them each a girl for a wife. Each son took his wife away and went home full of joy and contentment.

"So if you meet a man who is intelligent, wise, and good-natured, he is surely a descendant of the first girl, the daughter of man. If he is stupid and stubborn, then he must be descended from the offspring of the donkey. And if he shouts and weeps and wails and bemoans his fate for no reason at all, then he must be one of the descendants of the children of the dog. So you, dear listeners, will surely now know from whom this thief is descended!"

Shlomo ended his tale and resumed smoking the big *nargileh*, smiling into his moustache. The listeners praised Shlomo for the sweetness of his words, and the worthy sheikh exclaimed, "By Allah, your stories are sweet, O Mouth of Honey. They are even sweeter than the white sugar that is brought in sacks from the town!"

"And you, dear, honored sheikh," replied Shlomo, "if you would be so good as to heed my worthless advice, please let this young braggart go. Be lenient with him. He is the descendant of the dog. He is miserable and worthless. He has already learned his lesson, and I am sure that he will never again reap in other people's fields."

The elders and the notables praised Shlomo

for his wisdom and generosity. This is how a true man among men conducts himself!

The sheikh summoned the thief and told him of his decision. He would not be punished this time, but if he were ever caught again . . .

Tears of gratitude rolled down the rough cheeks of the young man, and he threw himself at Shlomo's feet and thanked him. Shlomo drew his feet away and said, "Get up, young man! It is beneath the dignity of a man to kiss another's feet, even if he is a descendant of the dog!"

The thief left the tent, his head submissively bowed, murmuring his thanks. Shlomo continued sitting among the elders, sipping coffee and drawing upon his *nargileh* until darkness fell and it was time to go home.

8
. . .

A Guest for the Festival

It was just before Passover. Some of the veteran settlers had met at Farmer Gafni's house to while away the rainy winter evening. They sat drinking hot coffee and spinning yarns about the approaching festival. One told a story about the prophet Elijah, a tale he had learned from his grandmother. Another described the seder night in an East European *shtetl*. Then Shlomo of Safad began to speak, and silence reigned immediately. Everyone knew that if the old "Horseman of Galilee" had something to say, there was probably a good story in the offing.

Shlomo of Safad came from an Ashkenazi family which had settled in Safad several hundred years previously and had never abandoned the town, despite the various misfortunes that befell the Jewish community there—the pogroms by the Druses, the earthquakes, the raids by gangs of thieves, and the sadistic whims of the Turkish government. Shlomo began his story:

"Let me tell you about something that happened to me one seder night. I see there are a few youngsters among the company tonight. It is for them that my story is especially intended.

"It happened when I first began working as a mounted watchman in upper Galilee, about forty years ago. The Turkish rule of Palestine had just ended. Chaos and lawlessness reigned throughout the land. Highwaymen haunted the roads, and travelers were in constant danger of losing their possessions and their lives.

"I was then a member of the Hashomer organization. A week before Passover we undertook the guarding of a settlement in upper Galilee near the Jordan River. The settlement was right in the center of a very dangerous area, one patrolled by thieves on horseback. These were predatory bedouins, looking for spoils abandoned by the retreating Turkish Army in its flight from the British and

the Australians. However, these bedouins had no hesitation about laying their hands on property that they were not entitled to in Jewish settlements. After they had been raided several times, the settlers had requested us to guard their lives and property against these predators. We worked hard the whole week. We placed armed guards around the perimeter of the settlement, and three times we caught thieves and robbers trying to break into Jewish farms to steal donkeys and oxen from the stables while the farmers slept.

"Then came seder night.

"When darkness fell, I shouldered my rifle and loaded my Mauser pistol, sticking it in my belt to be ready for a quick draw. I mounted my mare and set off on guard patrol.

"It was a clear night, but the moon had not yet risen. The festival lights had been lit in the settlement, and through the little windows of the houses I could see the tables covered with white tablecloths and carefully laid with the ritual dishes and shiny bottles of wine. The farmers, dressed in their best, sat at the table reading from the *Haggadah*, relating the story of the miracles performed for our forefathers thousands of years ago. Next to the head of the house sat his wife, dressed in her prettiest dress, and next to her sat the children, their eyes bright with expectation, waiting to steal the *afikomen* and receive a young colt to break in, in exchange. Everyone was singing and chanting the story of the exodus from Egypt. Only I, the lonely, solitary watchman, rode my horse among the rocks and boulders, expecting the bullet of an assassin to be lying in wait for me at any moment.

"My heart was heavy. I remembered the seder held every year at my home in Safad. The whole family would gather at my father's house, and I had never missed a single Passover at home. Now, for the first time, I was doomed to spend this festival night a long way from home.

"I rode among the houses, sheep pens, stables, and hen runs, pondering my fate sadly. Suddenly, I perceived a dim figure outlined against the

pale background of hillside. I halted my mare abruptly, surprised that she had given me no warning. Well-trained thoroughbred mares normally warn their riders of anything hidden in the darkness. My mare was a most excellent creature. Why had she not discerned the dim shape?

"In a flash I had drawn my Mauser. I released the safety catch and shouted in Arabic, '*Min hada*— Who's there?'

"There was no reply.

" 'Who's there?' I repeated in Hebrew, but still no one answered.

" 'If you don't say something, I'll shoot!' I shouted in Arabic.

"Then I heard a soft, calm, confident voice say, 'Don't shoot; I am not an enemy.'

"The dark shape approached, and in the dim light of the window of a nearby house I saw a tall old man, wrapped in a white prayer shawl and dressed in festive garb. He had a long white beard reaching to his cummerbund, and he wore sandals.

" 'Who are you?' I asked.

" 'I am Reb Zalman, a farmer from this settlement,' he replied.

"I did not recognize him, but then I had only been at the settlement a week, and had been so busy with the arduous task of guarding it, I had had little time to make the acquaintance of all the settlers.

" 'What are you doing here at this time of night?' I asked him.

"The old man was silent for a while. Then he said, 'I am quite alone in the world. I have no children, and my wife died many years ago. Every year I have guests for the festival, but this year, because of the raids, I have been left alone on seder night. Perhaps you, my son, would be my guest this time? The table is laid, the wine has been poured out, the unleavened bread is ready. Please come home with me!'

" 'Alas, I cannot, Reb Zalman,' I replied. 'To whom can I entrust the safety of the settlement?'

" 'Have no fear, my son,' the old man reassured me. 'Tonight is the night of the Vigil. The Rock of Israel keeps a vigil over His children on this night.'

" 'No, I musn't, Reb Zalman, I cannot abandon the settlement.'

" 'Nothing will happen tonight,' the old man repeated. 'In any case, my house is right at the edge of the settlement near the Jordan River. If the bedouins come, they will come from across the river, and we shall hear them.'

"I hesitated a little longer, but finally gave in. The old man had sounded so confident that he had managed to convince me.

"I followed the old man to the eastern edge

of the village. There stood a little whitewashed house surrounded by a neat fence. Light from the festival candles shone through the windows. I tethered my mare outside and entered. A little table stood in the center of the room. It had been laid for two people. All the requirements of Passover were set out on it. The old man seated himself in an armchair padded with white cushions and bade me sit next to him. He poured wine into the glasses and began to read from the *Haggadah* in a pleasant voice. 'We were slaves to pharaoh in Egypt . . .'

"Thus we passed the seder night the first night of Passover, the festival of spring and of freedom. The fragrance of plants and flowers and of the green wheat, which would soon ripen and yield golden grain, wafted in from outside. My heart was filled with happiness. The old man and I read the *Haggadah* together right through to the end. And the whole time I was certain, without being able to explain why, that the settlement was safe from marauders. The old man's presence filled me with confidence.

"When we had finished eating and reading from the *Haggadah*, I left the house. I mounted my mare and returned to my vigil; then I remembered that I had forgotten to thank the kind old farmer for his hospitality. I didn't want to abandon my rounds, so I decided to visit his house the next day to thank him for the wonderful seder he had held for me at his house."

At this point Shlomo, the veteran watchman, broke off his story to roll himself a new cigarette. With deft, measured movements he spread the shreds of tobacco along the length of the cigarette paper, rolled the paper around the tobacco, licked the paper along one edge, and stuck it down and lit it.

"Well, what happened? How does the story end?" asked Gadi, the host's eldest son, unable to contain his curiosity. "Did you thank the kind old man?"

"Patience, patience," replied the old watchman with a smile. "All in good time. Patience is as good for young people as the bridle is good for the mare."

"The next day," Shlomo finally continued, "I rode my mare down the path leading to the Jordan River toward the old man's house. I had a present for him which I had obtained from the watchmen's kitchen: sugar, wine, and potatoes— commodities worth their weight in gold in those hard times."

"Was the old man pleased with them?" asked Gadi.

The watchman paused for a moment, then stated slowly and dramatically. "I never saw the old man again. I did not find any house at the end of the path."

"How is it possible?" ejaculated Gadi.

"Well, it was possible. On the spot where the little house had stood, there was only a vacant, grassy plot. I asked the neighbors about Reb Zalman, and apparently there was no such farmer in the settlement, nor had there ever been."

"Amazing!" exclaimed Gadi. "But you ate the unleavened bread, didn't you? And you drank the wine? You ate Passover food?"

"Yes, indeed," replied the watchman. "In fact I can almost taste them on my tongue still."

"Perhaps . . . perhaps," stammered Gadi, "perhaps it was the prophet Elijah himself?"

"Perhaps," replied the old watchman, and said no more. He drew deeply on his cigarette, and a smile lingered beneath his thick, white moustache.

9

. . .

The Druse Mother

It was a chilly winter day. Heavy, gray clouds rolled down the mountainside from the west and unleashed their torrential rain. A cold wind blew across from the mountains of Lebanon, lashing my face and ruffling the mane of my mare, Tiferet. I had been riding the whole day. Tiferet's coat was wet, and steam rose from her flanks. Her tail was heavy with water, and rain streamed from her mane. My fingers were red and frozen with cold. The mare's hooves sank into the mud and made a squelching sound when she dragged them out. The path leading up the mountainside had turned into a small stream.

In the distance I could see the houses of the Druse village on the banks of the Hatzbani. The Hatzbani is one of the three sources of the Jordan River. It is situated in upper Galilee, close to the Lebanese border. My mare climbed the steep slope, her ears quivering. At the entrance to the village, we were buffeted by a fierce wind, and we progressed slowly and with difficulty.

The village was silent and still. Almost everyone was safe indoors. Here and there a Druse woman gathered her chickens into the hen run, her red dress blowing in the wind, and a young goatherd leaped from puddle to puddle, herding his flock into the pen.

It was the goatherd who told my Druse friend, Ismain El-Atrash, of my arrival. By the time I arrived at his house, he was awaiting me on the threshold. His eldest son took my mare away to the stable to be rubbed down and fed, and I entered the large, spacious guest room.

Ismain brought me a dry cloak, which I exchanged for my wet one, and spread a bearskin rug on the floor. The skin was from a bear he had killed himself in the mountains of Lebanon, and the fur was most comfortable to sit on.

Ismain is a hunter who tracks game in the mountains of Lebanon and the swamps of Huleh

Valley. He is a member of the famous El-Atrash family of which Sultan El-Atrash, the leader of the Druse rebellion against the French, is also a member.

I had met Ismain during the rebellion, when I spent some time in Jabal El-Druz, the Druse Mountain, the Druse territory in Syria where the rebellion took place. Since then we have been close friends.

Ismain's wife prepared the evening meal, and we sat around an iron stove filled with sizzling charcoal. We smoked our *nargilehs* and gulped down steaming hot strong black coffee from small blue china cups. His wife then brought a brass tray piled high with an assortment of delicacies. We ate heartily and thanked the housewife, then continued drinking the delicious coffee and smoking the *nargilehs*.

Meanwhile, the village elders had arrived, having heard that there was a visitor in their midst. They removed their wet cloaks and their shoes and seated themselves around the stove.

The coffeepot was passed around, and the smoke of the *nargilehs* curled upward. A red glow emanated from the charcoal and tinged the white beards of the village elders and Ismain's moustache. The room was warm, and the charcoal gave off a pleasant aroma.

Outside the wind blew down from the

mountains of Lebanon, howling and shrieking. The rain beat down upon the roofs, and streams of water gurgled down the gutters. Good coffee and fragrant *nargilehs* have a habit of encouraging pleasant conversation on a winter evening. The village elders told tales of the brave deeds of the Druses, particularly those performed during the great rebellion against the French.

While we sat and talked, the wind suddenly gave a terrible shriek, and from the mountains came a sound like the neighing of a horse. The sound rose, lasted for a few moments and died away in a prolonged, mournful wailing. The faces of the elders froze, and their wrinkled lips moved as they mumbled passages from psalms to the great and good God.

"It is the horse of Kamal of the house of Shehab," murmured one of them in an awed whisper.

"Kamal's horse is searching for a warm stable," added another. They fell silent and sat motionless.

"Who is Kamal Shehab?" I inquired.

No one answered. Ismain looked at me, twisting the ends of his big moustache, and finally said, "Yirmi, as a real friend of our people, I can tell you the story of Kamal of the house of Shehab, and of his mother, Sit El-Naifa, the proudest of women, and of his thoroughbred black horse. We Druses do not like to tell this story to strangers, for as you know, dear friend, among us bravery in battle is the ultimate virtue; the Druse is trained to be a warrior from his infancy. You see, this story is not about bravery, but rather . . . well, I'll begin and then you will understand for yourself."

Ismain paused for a moment, drank from his coffee cup, drew on his *nargileh*, and began his tale. "The Shehab family is famous for its brave and daring heroes. The men of the family are fearless warriors, expert in the use of the rifle, dagger, and revolver. They ride as if they and the horse were one being.

"Many legends are told of this family, which guards its honor most jealously. Any insult to it would meet with only one retort—bloodshed!

"For the Shehab family, honor and blood vengeance are of paramount importance. Just as their men are famous for their courage, so their womenfolk are renowned for their bravery, and they bring their sons up to be fighters and heroes. They make their sons strong and healthy and train them to be brave and daring. They never weep or mourn their nearest and dearest who fall in battle. They merely wear black and observe the mourning ritual. After all, if a man has died a hero's death, why weep for him? That is the way of a brave man. Lucky is the mother of such a son, or the wife of such a husband; she shall be praised among women.

"The story that I am about to tell you, my friend, happened during the great rebellion against the French, in the years immediately following the British conquest of Palestine. Syria, as you know, was conquered by the French. The French also tried to extend their rule over the Druse Mountain, but Druses do not lightly renounce their independence. They are lovers of freedom and hate foreign domination. So a rebellion broke out against the French. Bands of brave Druse fighters ambushed French soldiers and engaged them in battle.

"In those days a branch of the Shehab family lived in our village. The head of the family had been killed in the previous rebellion against the Turks and had left a wife, Sit El-Naifa, and one son, Kamal. Sit El-Naifa was a remarkable woman. She ran the family farm single-handedly, supervising the laborers and managing the ploughing, sowing, and reaping. She herself bargained with the merchants who came from town to buy the farm produce. She would walk through the village dressed in black, proud and erect as a cedar of Lebanon. She had raised her son, Kamal, by herself and had taught him to be courageous and daring. She had hired teachers to instruct him in the art of the sword and the rifle and had told him about his father, the famous hero, about whom songs of praise have been written and who was admired and respected by all. Naifa's son was everything to her. She loved him

most dearly, and it was for him that she worked so hard, so that he would grow into a fine youth, a man among men.

"The child grew into a quick, strong lad, agile and intelligent. When he was fifteen years old, his mother brought him a thoroughbred black colt from a strain of warhorses. This type of horse is the best there is. Its price is above gold. The boy and the

colt grew up together. The horse, being black, was
called Aswad. He became the swiftest and most excellent steed, a prize among horses.

"Kamal, riding his black horse, was a wonderful sight to see. The boy's green eyes flashed
with courage. He sat steadfast and erect in the saddle, a sword at his waist, a rifle slung over his shoulder, and two cartridge belts worn across his chest.
He was the proudest and bravest of riders. His gray-
haired mother would stand at the gateway of their
home and look at him, her eyes flashing with pride.
'Is there a woman happier than I?' she would ask
herself.

"Then the great rebellion came to all the
Druse villages of Palestine, Syria, and Lebanon.
Men leapt onto their horses and rode off to join the
rebels. They bade farewell to their mothers, kissed
their wives, embraced their children, and went off
to war.

"The old mother saddled Aswad with her
own hands. She herself tied the hunting saddlebag
and the water bottle to the saddle, attached a roll of
blankets to the back, cleaned Kamal's rifle,
sharpened his sword, and shined the reins. She said
to her son, 'Ride off, my boy. Go and fight. Be as
brave and strong as your father. One thing you
must know. No man of the Shehab family was ever
wounded in the back. No Shehab ever turned his
back on the enemy.'

"Kamal kissed his mother, bade her good-bye, and set off.

"Days and nights passed. The village was silent. In the houses the occupants waited for news of husbands, sons, brothers, and fathers. From time to time a horseman visited the village and the rumor would spread: 'So-and-so, the son of So-and-so, has gone the way of all men.' The village knew that if a man died in battle, his soul would enter the body of a newborn Druse male child, so what was the point of crying and mourning? This was wartime, and in war, casualties are inevitable.

"The proud Naifa did not go to hear news from the riders. 'If they have anything to tell me,' she would say to herself, 'they'll come to me. They will drink my coffee and tell me news of Kamal, my son, in my own house.'

"One cold, dark night, just like tonight, Naifa had finished her day's work and had taken up her needle and thread to embroider a new cloak for Kamal. Suddenly, there were two loud knocks at the door. Naifa froze in her chair. Who could it be so late at night? The knocking was repeated, firmly, but more softly."

Ismain paused for a moment. Everyone sat silent, listening intently. Those present had already heard the story many times, but no matter how often a good storyteller tells a tale, it always sounds new. And who could tell stories better than my

friend Ismain? He modulated his voice and deep-
ened it; then he would suddenly change to a whisper, make a dramatic pause, and resume his tale.

Ismain sipped his coffee, drew on his *nargileh*,
wiped his mouth, and took up the story again:

"Well, Naifa heard the knocking. Finally,
she rose, went to the door, and opened it. And there,
pale and ragged, weak and dusty, stood Kamal, her
son.

" 'Mother!' cried the boy.

" 'Kamal, my son!' exclaimed his mother,
'What has happened, Kamal? Why are you so pale?'

" 'Mother,' replied Kamal, 'there's no time to
lose. The French are on my tracks!'

" 'The French are on your tracks?'

" 'Yes, mother, they're after me!'

" 'And you are running away? Where are
your comrades?'

" 'Up there in the mountains. The French
have surrounded them. They'll all die. I alone
managed to escape on Aswad. Thanks to him, I am
safe. And now they are hunting me down like a
pack of wolves.'

"The old woman was frozen to the spot. It
was as if she had turned to stone.

" 'You ran away and left your friends to die
alone, without you?'

" 'Oh, mother, I didn't want to die in the
mountains!'

" 'You, your father's son, ran away? If only a bullet had hit your black horse, then you would have been spared this terrible shame.'

" 'Mother, mother, there's no time to waste. The French will be here soon. Hide me!'

"A mother is a mother, come what may. Naifa took Kamal up to the loft and hid him in the straw stored there. Then she led Aswad away to a neighbor, who would ride him around until daybreak. Finally she returned home to wait for the French.

"Finally they arrived, surrounded the house, searched everywhere, and questioned Kamal's mother. But she stood firm. 'My son has not been here, nor is his horse here.' The searchers finally gave up and rode away into the darkness.

"Then Naifa went and sat in her chair, silent and still, her hands clasped to her breast. Her son came down from the loft and went to his mother, but she said, 'No, don't come near me. Stay in the next room!'

"The boy obeyed like a little child and went into the next room. His mother sat there the whole night, but Kamal fell asleep on the carpet, worn out by his long ride.

"In the morning his mother woke him. 'Get up, wake up!' The boy arose. She brought him hot water.

" 'Wash yourself.' He washed his hands and

face. She brought him food. 'Eat!' He ate, ashamed
to look his mother in the face. When he had
finished, she told him to follow her.

"She led him into the courtyard, and there
stood his black horse, the saddlebags in place, and
the water bottle and blankets tied on.

" 'Mount!' she ordered.

" 'Where am I to go?" asked her son.

" 'Wherever you wish,' she replied. 'You are
no longer a member of the Druse race.'

" 'Mother,' implored Kamal, prostrating
himself at her feet.

" 'Get up!' she commanded. 'Do not humili-
ate yourself. Get up and mount your horse!'

" 'Mother,' wept the lad. 'I'll go back to war!'

" 'No!' she replied. 'Do you want to stain the
family's honor, which has been immaculate for gen-
erations? Each generation has added fresh glory to
the family name, and I shall not allow it to be dis-
graced—no, never! A family goes on for genera-
tions, even after you and I are dead. I don't want
people ever to say of the Shehab family: "Oh yes,
that was the family of that famous coward, Kamal
Shehab." Heaven preserve a family from such a son!
Go, mount your horse, my son. Ride off to wherever
you will. I never want to see your face again.'

" 'Mother, you loved me dearly. Where will
you send me?'

" 'Yes, I loved two people in my lifetime, and

I lost both of them: you and your father. When your father died, I did not weep, for he died a hero's death. And as for you, whom I loved so dearly, I lost you as well. But I shall not weep, for I am ashamed to. Because I loved you so dearly, I command you to go, for life without honor cannot be called life. Your place shall not be kept in your father's family.'

"The lad mounted his horse and rode out of the village. His mother stood watching her only son, whom she had loved dearly, until he disappeared down the path. And ever since"—Ismain ended his story—"ever since, Kamal has wandered through the mountains with no resting place. On dark, cold winter nights, he rides his horse, looking for food and warm shelter."

Ismain fell silent. The rain had stopped. The wind continued to howl and shriek around the rocks. Suddenly, from the mountains there rose a loud moaning, the sad and melancholy neigh of a horse, rising and falling, mingling with the sound of the wind. The elders muttered prayers and invocations. There was a muffled bubbling of the water in the *nargilehs* and the hiss of charcoal in the stove.

10

. . .

Scout Plane Over
the *Wadi*

Haim sat at his desk in the police station. The phone rang, and he lifted the receiver.

"Investigation Department. Haim speaking."

Chief Inspector Uzzieli was on the line. "Haim, come to my office immediately. It's something urgent."

Haim went off to Uzzieli's office. Uzzieli was a tall man whose hair was already streaked with gray. He always wore plain clothes, for uniforms would interfere with his work.

When Haim entered, Uzzieli was examining a large map of the Negev Desert. He pored over it, muttering to himself.

"Oh, is that you, Haim? Come in please."

Haim sat down.

"Listen, Haim," said Uzzieli, "I've just heard that there's a caravan of camels about, belonging to a drug-smuggling gang. They're moving along Wadi Abiad, the White *Wadi*. Do you know Mansur Abu Ahmed?"

"Yes, you mean the bedouin from the El-Rei'i tribe."

"That's the one. He is our informer in the area. He heard about the gang and sent us a carrier pigeon with the news."

"When did it arrive?"

"Just half an hour ago. The gang is already on its way. If we send police jeeps down there, they won't arrive in time."

"Yes, it's quite a way off."

"Listen, Haim, I must catch them. There's been too much smuggling lately."

Uzzieli fell silent and the pair sat deep in thought. Haim perused the note sent by the informer, Mansur Abu Ahmed. Mansur had once been a member of a smuggling gang himself, but he had quarreled with his confederates and they had expelled him from the gang. He established contact with the police and was willing to supply information for pay. Mansur would take a cage containing a carrier pigeon with him, and when the occasion arose, he would release the pigeon with a tiny box containing the pertinent information attached to its leg.

"There's very little time," urged Uzzieli. "We must act at once."

"I've got an idea," exclaimed Haim.

Haim was famous in the police force for his ingenuity, which had earned him the nickname "the Fox."

"Well, let's have it, Haim. Any idea is better than none."

"Is the police scout plane available?"

"Yes, it is."

"Then listen, Uzzieli. Put the scout plane at my disposal, and give me a Bren gun, grenades, and a loudspeaker. I'll fly down there, while you send police cars. There's no time to waste. We must get going immediately. I hope the plan works."

Uzzieli contacted the airfield north of the town and ordered the police pilot, Sergeant Moshiko, to get the plane ready for flight. Then he ordered a Bren gun, a full box of ammunition, and a loudspeaker from the police supplies. Outside, in the courtyard of the police station, a driver was already turning over the engine of a police jeep. Haim hopped in beside the driver.

"Good luck!" Uzzieli wished the police officer. "I don't know what your plan is, but I have complete faith in you."

The jeep made for the airfield at top speed.

In the meantime, police platoons had been alerted and mobilized in trucks and jeeps. The vehicles assembled in the courtyard. Their passengers, wearing battle dress, climbed in. The convoy set off for the south.

By this time the jeep carrying Haim had reached the airfield, which consisted of a single long gray runway. Sergeant Moshiko was already standing by the scout plane, a Piper Cub, whose cabin doors had been removed. Haim climbed out of the jeep, and with the help of the driver loaded the machine gun, ammunition, and loudspeaker into the plane. A police scout plane contains only two seats, one for the pilot and one behind it for a passenger.

Haim clambered onto the wing and entered the cabin. He sat in the passenger seat and fastened the safety belt. The pilot handed him several grenades which he placed on a shelf behind his head. He laid the machine gun across his knees and placed the box of ammunition beneath his seat. There was little room left for the loudspeaker. The pilot tied the amplifiers to the belly of the plane and attached

the microphone to Haim's seat. Then he hopped into his own seat and fastened his safety belt.

"Ready?" shouted the pilot.

"Ready," affirmed Haim.

"O.K., start her off!" shouted the pilot to the mechanic on the ground. The mechanic swung the propellers of the Piper Cub, and the plane's engine coughed into life. The hum of the engine grew louder as the pilot revved it up, while he checked the dials and switches on the instrument panel.

The noise of the engine drowned out everything else. The pilot signaled to the mechanic to remove the chocks behind the wheels, and when this had been done, he released the brake and gave the mechanic the takeoff signal.

"We're off!" he shouted to Haim.

The plane taxied, increasing speed. Haim gripped the heavy machine gun. Finally, the plane left the ground and began to gain height. It appeared to brush the roofs of the houses as it rose, but they soon fell away and the town looked like a child's toy.

Once in the air the noise of the engine seemed to decrease. The pilot contacted the base by radio and reported that the takeoff had been satisfactory. The pilot was also in radio contact with the police convoy moving south by road.

The Piper Cub flew over stretches of empty desert, bare limestone hills, dry gulches, and an occasional solitary bedouin riding his camel or a flock of sheep seeking food among the sparse vegetation. The pilot continued to fly southward, following the road that lay below him.

The terrain began to change. Now it was pitted with gullies and crevices. The White *Wadi* that ran through the middle of this region was so called because of its chalky soil, which made it look from the air like a long, white, meandering ribbon. The *wadi* was a most convenient trail for caravans of smugglers and contained many good hiding places.

The ribbon of the *wadi* came into view. Haim took out his telescope, pointed it out the cabin doorway, and surveyed the ground beneath him. The pilot flew lower, following the *wadi* from east to west. They passed over vegetation, boulders, white rock, and terrain crisscrossed with gorges and chasms. No one was in sight. The smugglers had apparently managed to penetrate deep into the territory and were approaching the Gaza Strip and the Egyptian border. (This was before the Six-Day War and the Gaza Strip was still part of Egypt.) Once they had crossed it, of course, there was no chance of capturing them.

The plane flew onward and approached the point where the *wadi* passed between rows of hills and rock-strewn plains. Then Haim spotted the camels. They were loaded with sacks and moved in what appeared to be a peaceful convoy. Actually, this was a group of dangerous, heavily armed smugglers. Their sacks contained hashish, a dangerous drug, which they were smuggling into Egypt via Israel from other Arab countries.

The plane circled above the caravan. The camel-riders, dressed in black cloaks, lifted their heads to look at the scout plane above them. In the plane's cabin, Haim fed a belt of ammunition into the machine gun and primed a number of grenades.

Suddenly, a loud, terrifying voice came from the belly of the plane, booming out in Arabic, "This is the Israeli police. This is the Israeli police! Stop the caravan. Stop the caravan! Don't move. Don't move!"

The camel-drivers could be seen clearly from the plane as they waved their hands about excitedly and struck their beasts. They were attempting to escape.

"Get ready for action," Haim warned the pilot.

The pilot turned the plane to a course that led him right above the caravan. Haim aimed and cocked the machine gun. He spoke into the loudspeaker, "Don't try to escape. Don't try to escape. We'll shoot anyone who runs away!"

The smugglers continued to ignore the warnings. They beat their camels and urged them on past the rocky hills, toward a place where the sides of the *wadi* grew steeper. If they managed to reach it, the high walls would prevent the plane from getting close to them. The scout plane dove sharply over the caravan with a loud whistle. Haim picked up a grenade and withdrew the pin. They were only ten meters above the camels' heads. Haim could see *keffiyehs* and cloaks flapping in the slip-stream of the aircraft. Haim threw the grenade, and it landed near the caravan with a loud explosion. The plane continued on course, and Haim aimed another grenade, which landed just ahead of the caravan. The camels stopped in fright and the smugglers were forced to halt, not knowing what they should do next.

"Look out!" cried the pilot. "One of them is pulling out a gun!"

Sure enough, a smuggler was struggling to pull a machine gun out of a long sack on his camel's back. Haim cocked the Bren gun, bracing the tripod against the sides of the cabin. He found the smuggler in the sights, while the smuggler was still wrestling to free his weapon. Haim aimed carefully and pulled the trigger. The plane's cabin filled with choking smoke from the gunpowder, and the vibrations from the gun shook the aircraft. The volley of machine-gun bullets raised small clouds of dust between the camels' legs. The smugglers were frozen

to the spot. The terrible voice boomed out again above them, "Hands up, hands up! Anyone trying to escape will be shot!"

Some riders still tried to make their getaway, but a new hail of bullets flew very close to the camels' legs, and finally the smugglers were forced to halt and raise their hands.

A strange sight met the first police vehicles to reach the spot. A group of men stood in the middle of the desert, their arms outstretched above them. Loaded camels wandered around them, and above them circled a Piper Cub scout plane, from which boomed a loud voice giving orders in Arabic.

SOME HEBREW AND ARABIC WORDS IN THIS BOOK

abu hamsa	type of rifle	ابو خمسة
afikomen	piece of unleavened bread hidden by the head of the house during the seder on Passover night; the children are sent to find it and demand a present as a "ransom" for its return	אֲפִיקוֹמָן
agal	band which holds the *keffiyeh* in place	عقال
aleikum salaam	peace be with you	عليكم السلام
Ashkenazi	Jews originally from France, Germany, or Eastern Europe, as opposed to the Sephardi, Jews who were originally of Spanish origin before their exile in 1492	אַשְׁכְּנַזִּי
aswad	black	أسود
azu	bedouin incursions	غزو
bakaratch	coffeepot	بكرج
bakshish	literally alms, but commonly used to mean a sum of money given as a reward or bribe	بخشيش
djinn	genie, spirit	جن
Druse	an Arabic-speaking non-Moslem people living in Syria, Lebanon, and Israel	درزي
etlauw	come out	اطلعو
fantasia	Arab celebration	فنتازيا
gefet	olive waste	גֶּפֶת
gom	blood vengeance	القتل
Haganah	underground Jewish defense army formed during the British Mandate over Palestine	הֲגָנָה
Haggadah	a book containing the liturgy for the seder service	הַגָּדָה
Hashomer	organization of Jewish youth who defended Jewish settlements	